THE BOOKS OF
EZRA AND NEHEMIAH

COMMENTARY BY

R. J. COGGINS

Lecturer in Old Testament Studies, King's College, London

CAMBRIDGE UNIVERSITY PRESS

CAMBRIDGE

LONDON · NEW YORK · MELBOURNE

Published by the Syndics of the Cambridge University Press
The Pitt Building, Trumpington Street, Cambridge CB2 1RP
Bentley House, 200 Euston Road, London NW1 2DB
32 East 57th Street, New York, NY 10022, USA
296 Beaconsfield Parade, Middle Park, Melbourne 3206, Australia

First published 1976

Printed in Great Britain
at the
University Printing House, Cambridge
(Euan Phillips, University Printer)

Library of Congress cataloguing in publication data
Bible. O.T. Ezra. English. New English. 1976.
The books of Ezra and Nehemiah.
(The Cambridge Bible commentary, New English Bible)
Bibliography: p.
Includes index.
1. Bible. O.T. Ezra – Commentaries.
2. Bible. O.T. Nehemiah – Commentaries.
I. Bible. O.T. Nehemiah. English. New English. 1976.
II. Coggins, R. J., 1929–
III. Title. IV. Series.
BS1353.C63   222'.7'077   75-26278
ISBN 0 521 08648 5 hard covers
ISBN 0 521 09759 2 paperback

GENERAL EDITORS' PREFACE

The aim of this series is to provide the text of the New English Bible closely linked to a commentary in which the results of modern scholarship are made available to the general reader. Teachers and young people have been especially kept in mind. The commentators have been asked to assume no specialized theological knowledge, and no knowledge of Greek and Hebrew. Bare references to other literature and multiple references to other parts of the Bible have been avoided. Actual quotations have been given as often as possible.

The completion of the New Testament part of the series in 1967 provides a basis upon which the production of the much larger Old Testament and Apocrypha series can be undertaken. The welcome accorded to the series has been an encouragement to the editors to follow the same general pattern, and an attempt has been made to take account of criticisms which have been offered. One necessary change is the inclusion of the translators' footnotes since in the Old Testament these are more extensive, and essential for the understanding of the text.

Within the severe limits imposed by the size and scope of the series, each commentator will attempt to set out the main findings of recent biblical scholarship and to describe the historical background to the text. The main theological issues will also be critically discussed.

Much attention has been given to the form of the volumes. The aim is to produce books each of which will be read consecutively from first to last page. The introductory material leads naturally into the text, which itself leads into the alternating sections of the commentary.

The series is accompanied by three volumes of a more general character. *Understanding the Old Testament* sets out to provide the larger historical and archaeological background, to say something about the life and thought of the people of the Old Testament, and to answer the question 'Why should we study the Old Testament?'. *The Making of the Old Testament* is concerned with the formation of the books of the Old Testament and Apocrypha in the context of the ancient near eastern world, and with the ways in which these books have come down to us in the life of the Jewish and Christian communities. *Old Testament Illustrations* contains maps, diagrams and photographs with an explanatory text. These three volumes are designed to provide material helpful to the understanding of the individual books and their commentaries, but they are also prepared so as to be of use quite independently.

P. R. A.
A. R. C. L.
J. W. P.

CONTENTS

MAP

THE FOOTNOTES TO THE
N.E.B. TEXT

The footnotes to the N.E.B. text are designed to help the reader either to understand particular points of detail – the meaning of a name, the presence of a play upon words – or to give information about the actual text. Where the Hebrew text appears to be erroneous, or there is doubt about its precise meaning, it may be necessary to turn to manuscripts which offer a different wording, or to ancient translations of the text which may suggest a better reading, or to offer a new explanation based upon conjecture. In such cases, the footnotes supply very briefly an indication of the evidence, and whether the solution proposed is one that is regarded as possible or as probable. Various abbreviations are used in the footnotes.

(1) Some abbreviations are simply of terms used in explaining a point: *ch(s).*, chapter(s); *cp.*, compare; *lit.*, literally; *mng.*, meaning; *MS(S).*, manuscript(s), i.e. Hebrew manuscript(s), unless otherwise stated; *om.*, omit(s); *or*, indicating an alternative interpretation; *poss.*, possible; *prob.*, probable; *rdg.*, reading; *Vs(s).*, Version(s).

(2) Other abbreviations indicate sources of information from which better interpretations or readings may be obtained.

Aq.　Aquila, a Greek translator of the Old Testament (perhaps about A.D. 130) characterized by great literalness.

Aram.　Aramaic – may refer to the text in this language (used in parts of Ezra and Daniel), or to the meaning of an Aramaic word. Aramaic belongs to the same language family as Hebrew, and is known from about 1000 B.C. over a wide area of the Middle East, including Palestine.

Heb.　Hebrew – may refer to the Hebrew text or may indicate the literal meaning of the Hebrew word.

Josephus　Flavius Josephus (A.D. 37/8–about 100), author of the *Jewish Antiquities*, a survey of the whole history of his people, directed partly at least to a non-Jewish audience, and of various other works, notably one on the *Jewish War* (that of A.D. 66–73) and a defence of Judaism (*Against Apion*).

Luc. Sept.　Lucian's recension of the Septuagint, an important edition made in Antioch in Syria about the end of the third century A.D.

Pesh.　Peshitta or Peshitto, the Syriac version of the Old Testament. Syriac is the name given chiefly to a form of Eastern Aramaic used by the Christian community. The translation varies in quality, and is at many points influenced by the Septuagint or the Targums.

Sam. Samaritan Pentateuch – the form of the first five books of the Old Testament as used by the Samaritan community. It is written in Hebrew in a special form of the Old Hebrew script, and preserves an important form of the text, somewhat influenced by Samaritan ideas.

Scroll(s) Scroll(s), commonly called the Dead Sea Scrolls, found at or near Qumran from 1947 onwards. These important manuscripts shed light on the state of the Hebrew text as it was developing in the last centuries B.C. and the first century A.D.

Sept. Septuagint (meaning 'seventy'); often abbreviated as the Roman numeral (LXX), the name given to the main Greek version of the Old Testament. According to tradition, the Pentateuch was translated in Egypt in the third century B.C. by 70 (or 72) translators, six from each tribe, but the precise nature of its origin and development is not fully known. It was intended to provide Greek-speaking Jews with a convenient translation. Subsequently it came to be much revered by the Christian community.

Symm. Symmachus, another Greek translator of the Old Testament (beginning of the third century A.D.), who tried to combine literalness with good style. Both Lucian and Jerome viewed his version with favour.

Targ. Targum, a name given to various Aramaic versions of the Old Testament, produced over a long period and eventually standardized, for the use of Aramaic-speaking Jews.

Theod. Theodotion, the author of a revision of the Septuagint (probably second century A.D.), very dependent on the Hebrew text.

Vulg. Vulgate, the most important Latin version of the Old Testament, produced by Jerome about A.D. 400, and the text most used throughout the Middle Ages in western Christianity.

[. . .] In the text itself square brackets are used to indicate probably late additions to the Hebrew text.

(Fuller discussion of a number of these points may be found in *The Making of the Old Testament* in this series.)

Table of events in the Persian period

Kings	Main Events
Cyrus 550–530	Cyrus' capture of Babylon 539
Cambyses 530–522	Persian conquest of Egypt 525
Darius I 522–486	Jerusalem temple rebuilt 520–515
Xerxes 486–465	
Artaxerxes I 465–424	
Darius II 423–404	Papyri from Elephantine (Egypt) 410–404
Artaxerxes II 404–358	Egypt regains independence 401
Artaxerxes III 358–338	
Darius III 336–330	Alexander the Great 336–323
	Persian power ended by battles of Issus (333) and Gaugamela (331)

For reasons explained in the commentary, it is not possible to date the work of Ezra and Nehemiah with certainty. The most probable dating is that Nehemiah began his work in 445 under Artaxerxes I and Ezra in 398 under Artaxerxes II, but alternative dates (Nehemiah 384 and Ezra 458) are also possible.

THE BOOKS OF

EZRA AND
NEHEMIAH

* * * * * * * * * * * * *

THE WORK OF THE CHRONICLER

In the volume in this series dealing with 1 and 2 Chronicles those books were described as 'a neglected work'. The reasons for this neglect are twofold: the fact that much of their contents can be paralleled elsewhere in the Old Testament, and the unattractiveness to us of the long lists of names which are so prominent a feature. When we come to Ezra and Nehemiah, the situation is very different. They deal with a period of history of which we have little knowledge from other sources, and they have therefore been given detailed attention so that we may find out as much as possible about an important but obscure epoch; and the lists of names – though still to be found – are less prominent here than in the earlier work.

It will be seen that the assumption is already being made that Ezra and Nehemiah should be linked with 1 and 2 Chronicles, and it is important to establish the nature of that link. The most obvious starting-point is to notice that the end of 2 Chronicles (36: 22–3) is repeated as the beginning of Ezra (1: 1–3a). All kinds of explanations for this repetition could be thought of, but the simplest remains the most likely – that the works were originally continuous; that Ezra and Nehemiah came to be regarded by the Jews as sacred scripture before Chronicles (Ezra–Nehemiah precede Chronicles in the Hebrew Bible); but when all were received as scripture, the link between the works was emphasized by the repetition of these

I

phrases. Further support for the view that regards Chronicles–Ezra–Nehemiah as essentially one single whole is provided by the fact that the apocryphal book 1 Esdras spans the period covered by the last chapters of 2 Chronicles and the book of Ezra, and is almost certainly dependent upon the canonical books, though the exact nature of the relationship is a complex question.

To these considerations can be added others of a more general kind. There are close linguistic similarities between Chronicles and Ezra–Nehemiah, and – though the point has been disputed – it is most likely that these point to common authorship. More important for our purposes in this commentary, there is a similarity of theological viewpoint to be found through the whole work. Since this must inevitably affect our judgement of much of the content of Ezra and Nehemiah, it needs to be set out more fully. Some further indication of the grounds for the views here set out will be found in the volume on 1 and 2 Chronicles (pp. 3–7).

It seems most likely that the Chronicler (the name customarily given to the author or authors of Chronicles–Ezra–Nehemiah) was active in Jerusalem, probably about the middle of the fourth century. (It has been suggested that Ezra was himself the Chronicler; but it seems more likely that the author looks back at Ezra's achievement from the viewpoint of a slightly later age.) For the Chronicler, it was at Jerusalem, and particularly in the temple, that God most especially showed his favour to his people, and so the whole work has the Jerusalem temple as its main focus of interest. The earlier history begins in detail only with David, and it is emphasized throughout that Jerusalem is the city of David. In this latter part of the work the emphasis is on continuity; that the newly rebuilt temple was on the same site as that which had been destroyed; that it was served by the same personnel, using the same sacred vessels. The whole community centred upon Jerusalem was, therefore, to see itself as the direct descendant of those who had received God's earlier promises.

The Chronicler's presentation of this thesis is by means of an extended survey of the nation's past, emphasizing those aspects which were of particular relevance to his own interests. We tend to think of such a presentation as 'historical', but the term may be somewhat misleading. Undoubtedly much historical information is contained within the work, but it should not be approached primarily as a history, or as a source of information about a particular period, but as a presentation of the kind of theological viewpoint which has just been outlined. Some consideration will be given later (pp. 5–8) to the historical problems associated with the books of Ezra and Nehemiah and this point will be seen to be of considerable importance.

THE AUTHOR'S USE OF SOURCES

Before any satisfactory consideration can be given to historical problems, however, it is necessary to examine in more detail the material underlying the books of Ezra and Nehemiah. The problem here is more complex than for 1 and 2 Chronicles, where it is clear that the underlying sources are for the most part to be found elsewhere in the Old Testament – parts of the Pentateuch, and the books of Samuel and Kings. There are no readily identifiable sources of this kind underlying Ezra and Nehemiah.

Nevertheless, it is generally agreed that these books cannot simply be taken as free compositions of a single author. Even a cursory glance through them will show that they contain what appear to be official documents, and that two substantial parts of the book of Ezra are written in Aramaic (4: 8 – 6: 18; 7: 12–26). This was a language closely akin to Hebrew, which came to replace Hebrew for everyday speech among the Jews in the last centuries B.C., and was also the language of Persian imperial records. There is, therefore, an inherent likelihood (which is to some extent borne out on closer examination) that the author had available to him material which may have originated from a kind of official archive, though the purpose to which he puts it is always his own. This point is seen with especial clarity in ch. 4, where Aramaic material from a number of periods has been brought together to illustrate the single theme of opposition to the loyal Jews. Another part of the Aramaic material, found in chs. 5 and 6, appears to form an alternative presentation of the rebuilding operations described in Hebrew in ch. 3.

The Hebrew sections of the two books also contain material which may have originated in quasi-official sources such as census-lists. This would apply to the lists of names in Ezra 2 (substantially repeated in Neh. 7) and in Neh. 11–12. In all these instances the essential point is that the author was able to use this material for his own overriding purpose of describing and accounting for the fortunes of the Jerusalem community.

Another problem of a similar kind concerns the relation of the first-person material in Nehemiah to the rest of the two books. This material is found in chs. 1–2; 4: 1 – 7: 5; 12: 27–43; and 13: 4–31. The difficulty here is twofold. First, it has in the past often been assumed, almost without question, that this can be regarded as a 'memoir' written by Nehemiah himself. But just as it is now commonly accepted that the stories about prophets in the Old Testament were written by their followers rather than by the prophets themselves, so it is more likely that this was written by someone else to do honour to Nehemiah, rather than representing his own 'diary'. It would have been put into the first person in a way that is common for such material both in the ancient world and today. (It was not many years ago that it was reported as remarkable of a British prime minister that he wrote his own speeches.) We should therefore keep this apologetic motive in mind when assessing the historical value of the first-person material.

The second difficulty in regard to these sections concerns their relation to the rest of the Chronicler's work. Many have taken the view that they are a later addition to the main body of the work, that the Nehemiah tradition existed separately

4

for a considerable time, and that the Chronicler's work should not be regarded as including the Nehemiah material in its 'first edition'. As will emerge at various points during the commentary, there is certainly a curious lack of relation between the material relating to Ezra and that concerned with Nehemiah, but we may not need to suppose a separate existence for the Nehemiah tradition, and the very complex editorial process which would thereby be involved; it may be better to suppose that here, as elsewhere, the Chronicler had sources available to him which have not always been fully incorporated in the main body of the work.

HISTORICAL PROBLEMS

1 and 2 Chronicles are rarely regarded by scholars as more than a secondary source of historical information for the period which they cover. Estimates of their historical reliability have varied very greatly, but if the view taken here and in the companion volume dealing with 1 and 2 Chronicles is correct, the main purpose of the Chronicler was to set out the religious point of view explained above rather than to write accurate history. When we come to Ezra and Nehemiah the position is very different. Now there are no longer alternative sources of information available for the greater part of the period covered, and these books supply us with much of what we know, and present considerable problems.

From extra-biblical sources we know that the Babylonian Empire, virtually founded by Nebuchadnezzar, was short-lived. By 539 B.C., it had collapsed, and power had passed into the hands of Cyrus, the ruler of Persia. Persian rule was rapidly consolidated in Palestine and as far as the borders of Egypt. For a time Egypt itself was under Persian control. The Persians on various occasions unsuccessfully attempted to extend their rule into Europe, but though these attempts were thwarted, they remained in undisputed control of the whole of south-western Asia until the spread of Greek power by

Alexander the Great, who ruled from 336 to 323 B.C. It is within this overall context of Persian rule (539–336) that the events described in Ezra and Nehemiah took place. (See Table of events, p. xi.)

Many historical problems arise in the study of these books, and some attention will be given to the chief ones in the commentary, but there are two matters which have been the subject of much discussion and may appropriately be noted here. The first concerns the period of the rise of Persian power, and the events described in Ezra 1–3. It is clear that permission was given for the rebuilding of the temple and this meant that Jerusalem could resume something of its old role as a cult centre. It is much less clear whether Persian policy envisaged a substantial return of those who had been deported from their homelands. Two forms of the decree of Cyrus are found in Ezra (1: 2–4 and 6: 3–5). The latter, which is in the Aramaic section of the book, is concerned only with the temple rebuilding; the former, in Hebrew, also authorizes a large-scale return to Palestine. Since we have no supporting evidence of such a migration, which is not suggested by the books of Haggai and Zechariah, which also date from this period, it may well be that this is an idealization by the Chronicler. For him, it was inevitable that the exiled congregation should have taken the first opportunity to return to their homeland; the reality may have been much less exciting, with greater freedom of movement allowed under the Persian régime, but nothing corresponding to the movement of many thousands of people as described in Ezra 2.

The other historical problem concerns a period somewhat later. It is that of the chronological order of Ezra and Nehemiah. At first sight, the Old Testament seems to provide a clear answer. Since both are placed in the reign of Artaxerxes (Ezra 7: 7; Neh. 2: 1), it appears that – assuming the Persian king Artaxerxes I (465–424 B.C.) is meant – Ezra can be dated at 458 B.C. and Nehemiah at 445 B.C. The assumption that the references are to the same Persian king has, however, been widely questioned, and many scholars, perhaps a majority, have felt that Ezra should be placed after Nehemiah, in the reign of Artaxerxes II (404–358 B.C.), i.e. around 398 B.C. The grounds for such a view are mainly the curious lack of cross-references between the descriptions of the work of Ezra and of Nehemiah although as the biblical text now stands Ezra is envisaged as carrying out his task of proclaiming the Law at the time when Nehemiah was governor (Neh. 8). In support of this reversal of order a number of details have been adduced, such as the likely succession of high priests (see the commentary on Ezra 10: 6), and the general impression created by the text that Nehemiah was carrying out a pioneering work, whereas Ezra was preaching to an established community.

An answer on these lines may well be correct, but it is important to recognize that we have no real supporting evidence from other sources which enables us to date either Ezra or Nehemiah. Certainly neither of them is mentioned by name in extra-biblical sources. It has, indeed, commonly been assumed that we have one piece of evidence which makes Nehemiah's date almost certain at 445 B.C. Early in this century, a number of texts written on papyrus were discovered at Elephantine, near Aswan in Egypt, which referred to the life of a Jewish colony there. Among these texts were references to 'Delaiah and Shelemaiah the sons of Sanballat the governor of Samaria'. This text dates from about 408 B.C., and the assumption has commonly been made that Sanballat – active nearly forty years earlier, at the time of Nehemiah – was now an old man who left his sons to carry out the duties of governorship. This may indeed be the case, but the position has been complicated by other texts, the so-called 'Samaria papyri', which mention the existence of another Sanballat as governor in the fourth century. Some scholars have argued that Nehemiah's mission should be dated in the time of Artaxerxes II, that is, from about 384 B.C. onwards. This would be another way of explaining the lack of cross-reference between the two leaders.

Finally, the possibility of retaining the traditional dating – Ezra in 458, Nehemiah in 445 – should not be excluded. The lack of cross-reference between the two men may be more of a problem for us than it was for the ancient writer, and we are reminded of the lack of any reference between other Old Testament figures who were contemporaries – Jeremiah and Ezekiel, for example. If the sources of information about Ezra and Nehemiah were originally separate, it is perfectly possible that each concentrates on its own presentation of events without reference to the part played by others. If this is so, the passages which refer to both men together (e.g. Neh. 8: 9) would be later glosses, but would nevertheless give the right sense.

It seems best, therefore, to admit that we do not know the answer to the question of precedence. If a reconstruction must be attempted, then that which places Nehemiah in 445 and Ezra in 398 may be the least unsatisfactory, but we have seen that each date is open to challenge, and it is better to admit frankly that the materials for a precise reconstruction are not available to us.

Following on from this, a more general caution may usefully be made. As has already been observed, the books of Ezra and Nehemiah often provide the only information we possess about the period they cover. Compared with later presentations of the same period they are obviously more reliable historical witnesses, as may be seen, for example, by a comparison with the picture in 2 Maccabees 1 and 2 of the work of Nehemiah, where he is described as having 'built the temple and the altar' (2 Macc. 1: 18). A moment's reflection will show, however, that this greater reliability in no way implies absolute historical trustworthiness, and – just as in the rest of the Chronicler's work – we may expect to find a theological motivation underlying many apparently historical statements. In short, the same caution with regard to historical reconstruction that is commonly accorded to 1 and 2 Chronicles is also necessary here.

✳   ✳   ✳   ✳   ✳   ✳   ✳   ✳   ✳   ✳   ✳   ✳   ✳   ✳   ✳   ✳

THE BOOK OF

EZRA

✻ ✻ ✻ ✻ ✻ ✻ ✻ ✻ ✻ ✻ ✻ ✻ ✻ ✻ ✻ ✻

The return of the exiles to Jerusalem

THE LORD'S FAVOUR SHOWN THROUGH CYRUS

NOW IN THE FIRST YEAR of Cyrus king of Persia, so **1**
that the word of the LORD spoken through Jeremiah
might be fulfilled, the LORD stirred up the heart of Cyrus
king of Persia; and he issued a proclamation throughout
his kingdom, both by word of mouth and in writing, to
this effect:

This is the word of Cyrus king of Persia: The LORD **2**
the God of heaven has given me all the kingdoms of the
earth, and he himself has charged me to build him a
house at Jerusalem in Judah. To every man of his people **3**
now among you I say, God be with him, and let him
go up to Jerusalem in Judah, and rebuild the house of
the LORD the God of Israel, the God whose city is
Jerusalem. And every remaining Jew, wherever he may **4**
be living, may claim aid from his neighbours in that
place, silver and gold, goods*a* and cattle, in addition to
the voluntary offerings for the house of God in
Jerusalem.

Thereupon the heads of families of Judah and Benjamin, **5**

[a] *Or* pack-animals.

9

and the priests and the Levites, answered the summons,
all whom God had moved to go up to rebuild the house
6 of the LORD in Jerusalem. Their neighbours all assisted
them with gifts of every kind, silver[a] and gold, goods[b]
and cattle and valuable gifts in abundance,[c] in addition to
7 any voluntary service. Moreover, Cyrus king of Persia
produced the vessels of the house of the LORD which
Nebuchadnezzar had removed from Jerusalem and placed
8 in the temple of his god; and he handed them over into
the charge of Mithredath the treasurer, who made an
inventory of them for Sheshbazzar the ruler of Judah.
9 This was the list: thirty gold basins, a thousand silver
10 basins, twenty-nine vessels of various kinds, thirty golden
bowls, four hundred and ten silver bowls of various types,
11 and a thousand other vessels. The vessels of gold and
silver amounted in all to five thousand four hundred; and
Sheshbazzar took them all up to Jerusalem, when the
exiles were brought back from Babylon.

* Ezra 1 is properly understood as the sequel to 2 Chron. 36,
according to which all 'who escaped the sword he [Nebuchad-
nezzar] took captive to Babylon' (verse 20), while the land lay
desolate. For the Chronicler, that is to say, the true community was to be found in Babylon, and the picture given
here and more fully developed in succeeding chapters is of the
continuing kindness of the LORD toward them. When the
punishment is complete, they are allowed to return to their
homeland, the sacred vessels are restored to them, protection
against enemies is given to allow the rebuilding of the temple,

[a] with gifts...silver: *prob. rdg.*, *cp. 1 Esdras 2: 9*; *Heb.* with vessels of
silver.
[b] *Or* pack-animals.
[c] in abundance: *prob. rdg.*, *cp. 1 Esdras 2: 9*; *Heb.* apart.

and the city of David can again take its rightful place as the
centre of the divine presence with the chosen people. To such
generosity on the part of its God, the community is pictured
as responding willingly and promptly, and much of the
material is shaped to bring out this twofold picture of divine
initiative and human response.

1–3*a*. These verses are found also at the end of 2 Chronicles,
where they are broken off in the middle of the decree of
Cyrus. Here they are in their more natural context.

1. *in the first year of Cyrus:* he had already ruled for some
years over Persia and Media, but the important consideration
for the Chronicler was his rule over the former Babylonian
Empire, which began in 539/8 B.C. *the word of the LORD
spoken through Jeremiah:* internal cross-references of this kind
in the Old Testament are not frequent, and it is not certain
which passage is here being referred to – the book of Jeremiah
contains promises both of the end of the exile (Jer. 29: 10) and
of the rebuilding of Jerusalem (Jer. 31: 38). An allusion to the
words in the book of Isaiah referring to Cyrus (Isa. 44: 28 –
45: 1) may also be intended. There are in fact a number of
sections in Ezra where it appears as if the poetic language
concerning restoration and salvation of Isa. 40–55 is used as
the basis for factual statement. *the LORD stirred up the heart of
Cyrus:* two points are here made: the initiative is firmly
ascribed to the LORD's own activity; and a very positive role
is given to the Persian kings. This favourable attitude to the
Persian rulers is found throughout Ezra and Nehemiah.

2–4. There has been much dispute about the genuineness of
Cyrus' 'proclamation', both in its Hebrew form here and in
the Aramaic version found in ch. 6. Cyrus himself never was a
Yahweh-worshipper, but it is possible that the ascription of
his success to *The LORD the God of heaven* is due to the fact
that this version of a decree issued to a number of peoples was
prepared by a Jewish exile. On the other hand, it is perhaps
more likely that this form of the decree, with its emphasis on
permission to *go up to Jerusalem*, unparalleled as far as we know

elsewhere, may be a free composition of the Chronicler. It is instructive to compare this 'proclamation' with the Cyrus Cylinder, now in the British Museum, in which Cyrus ascribes his victories to the Babylonian god Marduk, and speaks of restoring captive gods to their various sanctuaries: 'the gods whose abode is in the midst of them, I returned to their places and housed them in lasting abodes'. (On the Cyrus Cylinder, see *Old Testament Illustrations* in this series, pp. 94f.)

5. *Thereupon:* the N.E.B. introduces this word, which has no precise equivalent in the Hebrew text, but it well illustrates the sense of urgency of the Chronicler's account. *Judah and Benjamin:* this corresponds with the picture in 2 Chron. (11: 1 and elsewhere) of these as the only loyal tribes, but is somewhat at variance with the Chronicler's emphasis elsewhere on 'all Israel'.

6. *Their neighbours all assisted them with gifts:* this is a good example of an apparently 'historical' statement whose real significance is probably quite different. This is surely intended as a deliberate allusion to, and comparison with, Exod. 11: 2 and 12: 35, the 'spoiling of the Egyptians'. Here as elsewhere, a theme found in Isa. 40–55 is picked up; the prophet had there envisaged the return from Babylon in terms of the exodus from Egypt (e.g. Isa. 51: 10f.) and that comparison is now spelt out.

7. *Cyrus king of Persia produced the vessels:* this may also be understood as a transformation of a poetic vision in Isaiah (52: 11) into a statement of fact, but in this case major historical difficulties stand in the way of our accepting it as such. According to 2 Kings 24: 13 the Babylonians 'broke up all the vessels of gold'. It seems likely that the point being made by the Chronicler is an emphasis on continuity between the former temple and the new one about to be built on its old site and – so he claimed – with the same vessels available. The theme was developed still further in later writings, notably the story of Belshazzar's feast in Daniel 5.

8. *Mithredath the treasurer:* otherwise unknown, but his name is in a characteristically Persian form. *Sheshbazzar the ruler of Judah:* a problem is posed by this apparently important figure, who is pictured here as having charge of the vessels and in 5: 16 as playing a major role in the return and the laying of the temple foundations. His role is to some extent duplicated by that of Zerubbabel in other traditions, but neither the suggestion that they are different names for the same person, nor the attempt to identify Sheshbazzar with some other figure of the period (e.g. Shenazzar, the uncle of Zerubbabel, according to 1 Chron. 3: 18), is satisfactory. Here, as elsewhere, more than one source was available to the Chronicler, and no systematic attempt at harmonization of this kind of detail has been made.

9–11. There are some difficulties in this list both of translation (some of the terms used are of uncertain meaning) and from the fact that the total does not correspond with the sum of the parts. It is impossible now to reconstruct the original form of the list with confidence; we may simply note that the difficulty was felt as long ago as the time of the Greek translation (the apocryphal book 1 Esdras), where the numbers are harmonized so that the total there does agree with the sum of the parts. *took them all up:* the emphasis is on completeness – *all* the vessels, accompanied by all the faithful community. *

THE LIST OF THOSE WHO RETURNED

Of the captives whom Nebuchadnezzar king of Baby- **2** 1[a]
lon had taken into exile in Babylon, these were the people
of the province who returned to Jerusalem and Judah,
each to his own city, led by Zerubbabel, Jeshua,[b] Nehe- 2
miah, Seraiah, Reelaiah, Mordecai, Bilshan, Mispar,
Bigvai, Rehum and Baanah.

The roll of the men of the people of Israel: the family 3

[a] *Verses 1–70: cp. Neh. 7: 6–73.*   [b] *Or Joshua (cp. Hag. 1: 1).*

13

of Parosh, two thousand one hundred and seventy-two;

4 the family of Shephatiah, three hundred and seventy-two;

5, 6 the family of Arah, seven hundred and seventy-five; the family of Pahath-moab, namely the families of Jeshua

7 and[a] Joab, two thousand eight hundred and twelve; the family of Elam, one thousand two hundred and fifty-four;

8, 9 the family of Zattu, nine hundred and forty-five; the

10 family of Zaccai, seven hundred and sixty; the family of

11 Bani, six hundred and forty-two; the family of Bebai, six

12 hundred and twenty-three; the family of Azgad, one

13 thousand two hundred and twenty-two; the family of

14 Adonikam, six hundred and sixty-six; the family of

15 Bigvai, two thousand and fifty-six; the family of Adin,

16 four hundred and fifty-four; the family of Ater, namely

17 that of Hezekiah, ninety-eight; the family of Bezai, three

18 hundred and twenty-three; the family of Jorah, one hun-

19 dred and twelve; the family of Hashum, two hundred and

20, 21 twenty-three; the family of Gibbar, ninety-five. The

22 men[b] of Bethlehem, one hundred and twenty-three; the

23 men of Netophah, fifty-six; the men of Anathoth, one

24 hundred and twenty-eight; the men of Beth-azmoth,[c]

25 forty-two; the men of Kiriath-jearim,[d] Kephirah, and

26 Beeroth, seven hundred and forty-three; the men[e] of

27 Ramah and Geba, six hundred and twenty-one; the men

28 of Michmas, one hundred and twenty-two; the men of

29 Bethel and Ai, two hundred and twenty-three; the men[f]

[a] and: *prob. rdg., cp. Neh. 7: 11; Heb. om.*
[b] *Prob. rdg., cp. Neh. 7: 26; Heb.* family.
[c] *Prob. rdg., cp. Neh. 7: 28; Heb.* the family of Azmoth.
[d] *Prob. rdg., cp. Neh. 7: 29; Heb.* the family of Kiriath-arim.
[e] *Prob. rdg., cp. Neh. 7: 30; Heb.* family.
[f] *Prob. rdg.; Heb.* family (*also in verses 30–5*).

of Nebo, fifty-two; the men of Magbish, one hundred 30
and fifty-six; the men of the other Elam, one thousand 31
two hundred and fifty-four; the men of Harim, three 32
hundred and twenty; the men of Lod, Hadid, and Ono, 33
seven hundred and twenty-five; the men of Jericho, three 34
hundred and forty-five; the men of Senaah, three thou- 35
sand six hundred and thirty.

Priests: the family of Jedaiah, of the line of Jeshua, nine 36
hundred and seventy-three; the family of Immer, one 37
thousand and fifty-two; the family of Pashhur, one thou- 38
sand two hundred and forty-seven; the family of Harim, 39
one thousand and seventeen.

Levites: the families of Jeshua and Kadmiel, of the line 40
of Hodaviah, seventy-four. Singers: the family of Asaph, 41
one hundred and twenty-eight. The guild of door- 42
keepers: the family of Shallum, the family of Ater, the
family of Talmon, the family of Akkub, the family of
Hatita, and the family of Shobai, one hundred and thirty-
nine in all.

Temple-servitors:[a] the family of Ziha, the family of 43
Hasupha, the family of Tabbaoth, the family of Keros, 44
the family of Siaha, the family of Padon, the family of 45
Lebanah, the family of Hagabah, the family of Akkub,
the family of Hagab, the family of Shamlai,[b] the family of 46
Hanan, the family of Giddel, the family of Gahar, the 47
family of Reaiah, the family of Rezin, the family of 48
Nekoda, the family of Gazzam, the family of Uzza, the 49
family of Paseah, the family of Besai, the family of Asnah, 50
the family of the Meunim,[c] the family of the Nephusim,[d]

[a] *Heb*. Nethinim.   [b] *Or* Shalmai (*cp. Neh.* 7: 48).
[c] *Or* Meinim.   [d] *Or* Nephisim.

51 the family of Bakbuk, the family of Hakupha, the family
52 of Harhur, the family of Bazluth, the family of Mehida,
53 the family of Harsha, the family of Barkos, the family of
54 Sisera, the family of Temah, the family of Neziah, and
the family of Hatipha.

55 Descendants of Solomon's servants: the family of
Sotai, the family of Hassophereth, the family of Peruda,
56 the family of Jaalah, the family of Darkon, the family of
57 Giddel, the family of Shephatiah, the family of Hattil, the
family of Pochereth-hazzebaim, and the family of Ami.

58 The temple-servitors and the descendants of Solomon's
servants amounted to three hundred and ninety-two in
all.

59 The following were those who returned from Tel-
melah, Tel-harsha, Kerub, Addan, and Immer, but could
not establish their father's family nor whether by descent
60 they belonged to Israel: the family of Delaiah, the family
of Tobiah, and the family of Nekoda, six hundred and
61 fifty-two. Also of the priests: the family of Hobaiah, the
family of Hakkoz, and the family of Barzillai who had
married a daughter of Barzillai the Gileadite and went by
62 his[a] name. These searched for their names among those
enrolled in the genealogies, but they could not be found;
63 they were disqualified for the priesthood as unclean, and
the governor forbade them to partake of the most sacred
food until there should be a priest able to consult the
Urim and the Thummim.

64 The whole assembled people numbered forty-two
65 thousand three hundred and sixty, apart from their slaves,
male and female, of whom there were seven thousand

[a] *Prob. rdg., cp. 1 Esdras 5: 38; Heb.* their.

three hundred and thirty-seven; and they had two hundred singers, men and women. Their horses numbered 66 seven hundred and thirty-six, their mules two hundred and forty-five, their camels four hundred and thirty-five, 67 and their asses six thousand seven hundred and twenty.

When they came to the house of the LORD in Jerusalem, 68 some of the heads of families volunteered to rebuild the house of God on its original site. According to their 69 resources they gave for the fabric fund a total of sixty-one thousand drachmas of gold, five thousand minas of silver, and one hundred priestly robes.

The priests, the Levites, and some of the people lived in 70 Jerusalem and its suburbs;*[a]* the singers, the door-keepers, and temple-servitors,*[b]* and all other Israelites, lived in their own towns.

* This lengthy list of names is reminiscent of the beginning of the Chronicler's work, though on this occasion it is not a genealogy, but a series of lists put together and then represented as being those who returned from Babylon with Sheshbazzar. A slightly different form of the same list is found in Neh. 7. The origin of the list is unknown – it has often been suggested that it may represent some form of census, though its varied nature (see commentary below) renders that suggestion doubtful. It is most unlikely that it refers to a list of those who in fact returned from Babylon – as we have seen, such a mass return is improbable – but it enables the Chronicler to provide a vivid illustration of the point he is making, about the people's faithfulness to the divine command and their eagerness to restore the holy city.

2. There are eleven names here, but twelve in the corres-

[a] in Jerusalem and its suburbs: *prob. rdg., cp. 1 Esdras 5: 46; Heb. om.*
[b] *Prob. rdg.; Heb. adds* in their towns.

17

ponding verse in Nehemiah (7: 7). Perhaps they are to be pictured as leaders of the twelve tribes. A possible origin of this group would be that it is actually a list of those who were known leaders of Judah during the period from the time of Cyrus to the Chronicler's own day: Zerubbabel and Jeshua are frequently referred to elsewhere; Nehemiah could be the governor after whom the book is named; there was a Persian governor of Judah called Bigvai at the time of the Elephantine papyri (late fifth century; cp. p. 7). The correspondence of names might be coincidental, but in any case the absence of any reference to Sheshbazzar is noteworthy – the traditions which mention him are always separate from those in which Zerubbabel appears.

3-19. The first major section of *The roll...of the people of Israel* (note this usage here, as against the 'Judah and Benjamin' of ch. 1) takes the form of lists of families. In addition to the parallel version of the list in Neh. 7, a further variant is found in a list of 'chiefs of the people' in Neh. 10: 14-19. It is clear that these families played a prominent part in the Jerusalem community of the Chronicler's time or a little earlier, but we have no other knowledge of them. Their names are a mixture of indigenous forms with Babylonian and Persian names, only two being compounded with 'Yahweh' (such names usually bear the suffix '-iah' in English).

20-1. It is not clear where the change from family- to place-name listing begins. In the Hebrew text both Gibbar and Bethlehem are counted as families; the N.E.B. has altered the second but not the first (see footnote). It is probable that *Gibbar* should be modified to 'Gibeon' as in Neh. 7: 25, and regarded as the beginning of the next section, a view which is rendered more likely because the correspondence with the list in Neh. 10 ends with 'Hashum'.

21-35. This grouping consists of inhabitants of particular places (though, as the N.E.B. footnotes indicate, the Hebrew text in several places reverts to the use of 'family of' rather than 'men of'). Not all the places named can be certainly identified, but the majority of them are in Benjamite territory, north of Jerusalem. As the list stands, it is not possible to trace any principle of grouping of the various places named.

36–9. Priests are here listed. The arrangement of the whole chapter, classifying the community as Israelites, priests and Levites, is an important indication of the way in which many later lists, right down into the Christian era, were to classify Israelite society, no longer as a nation but as a religious community. Of the names here mentioned, Jedaiah, Immer and Harim are mentioned among the priestly families of 1 Chron. 24; Pashhur is not there listed, though there is a well-known priest of the same name in Jer. 20: 1–6.

40–2. The numbers of Levites are much smaller, as is regularly the case in these lists. This is the more so, if (against the N.E.B. paragraphing) *Singers* and *door-keepers* are regarded as being listed separately. It may well be that it was not until some time after the establishment of the second temple that the role of the Levites was precisely defined.

43–54. The *Temple-servitors* are listed by families without any detailed indication of numbers; their menial position may well have meant that they were not strictly to be included within the ranks of Israel, and so only a summary total is given (verse 58). As the N.E.B. footnote indicates, the word translated *temple-servitors* is *nethinim*, literally 'given ones'. The names here found suggest that they may have been of foreign extraction, but were nevertheless 'given' to the service of the true God and his temple.

55–7. This group of *Descendants of Solomon's servants* appears to be related to the 'temple-servitors' of the preceding section from the fact that one numerical total is given for the combined list, but we know nothing of their origin.

59–63. These verses bring out an important concern of the Chronicler. From the outset of his work, in 1 Chron. 1–9, he has stressed the importance of being able to establish a genealogy as showing membership of the true community, and those unable to establish their descent are listed separately as not partaking of all the privileges of that community. Those listed in verse 60 are lay Israelites; in verse 61, claimants to the priesthood. The places named in verse 59 are not identifiable, though the prefix *Tel-* for the first two suggests the artificial mounds in Mesopotamia which were so described.

63. *the governor forbade them to partake of the most sacred food:* it is noteworthy that the decision is taken by the governor. The word here used – *tirshatha* – is applied to Nehemiah (Neh. 8: 9; 10: 1) but is not the same word as is used of Zerubbabel in Haggai (1: 1 and elsewhere). Since we have no means of dating the lists here, we cannot tell who is being referred to, but it is noteworthy that he is envisaged as controlling the religious as well as the secular affairs of the community. The particular disqualification mentioned involved the priestly part of the sacrifices of the temple. *a priest able to consult the Urim and the Thummim:* the restoration is pictured as incomplete, and one of the marks of its completion would be the emergence of a priest able to carry out all the duties laid down in the law – this is one of the few signs of the Chronicler's future expectations. The Urim and Thummim were originally some form of oracular device, which gave two (or perhaps three) forms of answer, positive, negative and uncertain; by this period it would seem that they were simply an ornamental feature of the priestly robes (cp. Exod. 28: 30), and here the hope is expressed that they will one day come into use once more.

64. The numbers here given do not correspond to the component parts of the list, but material of this kind is notoriously liable to corruption in transmission.

69. The wealth here said to be available is in very marked contrast to the poverty of the community pictured in the contemporary prophecy of Haggai (cp. Appendix, p. 147).

70. In the Hebrew this verse is almost unintelligible; possibly it represents the link between the list and the narration which now follows. *

Worship restored and the temple rebuilt

RESTORATION BEGUN

WHEN THE SEVENTH MONTH CAME, the Israelites **3**
now being settled in their towns, the people
assembled as one man in Jerusalem. Then Jeshua son of 2
Jozadak and his fellow-priests, and Zerubbabel son of
Shealtiel and his kinsmen, set to work and built the altar
of the God of Israel, in order to offer upon it whole-
offerings as prescribed in the law of Moses the man of
God. They put the altar in place first, because they lived 3
in fear of the foreign population; and they offered upon
it whole-offerings to the LORD, both morning and
evening offerings. They kept the pilgrim-feast of Taber- 4
nacles[a] as ordained, and offered whole-offerings every
day in the number prescribed for each day, and, in addi- 5
tion to these, the regular whole-offerings and the offerings for sabbaths,[b] for new moons and for all the sacred
seasons appointed by the LORD, and all voluntary
offerings brought to the LORD. The offering of whole- 6
offerings began from the first day of the seventh month,
although the foundation of the temple of the LORD had
not yet been laid. They gave money for the masons and 7
carpenters, and food and drink and oil for the Sidonians
and the Tyrians to fetch cedar-wood from the Lebanon

[a] *Or* Booths.
[b] for sabbaths: *prob. rdg., cp. 1 Esdras 5: 52; Heb. om.*

to the roadstead at Joppa, by licence from Cyrus king of Persia.

8 In the second year after their return to the house of God in Jerusalem, and in the second month, Zerubbabel son of Shealtiel and Jeshua son of Jozadak started work, aided by all their fellow-Israelites, the priests and the Levites and all who had returned from captivity to Jerusalem. They appointed Levites from the age of twenty years and upwards to supervise the work of the house of the LORD.

9 Jeshua with his sons and his kinsmen, Kadmiel, Binnui, and Hodaviah,*a* together assumed control of those responsible for the work on the house of God.*b*

10 When the builders had laid the foundation of the temple of the LORD, the priests in their robes took their places with their trumpets, and the Levites, the sons of Asaph, with their cymbals, to praise the LORD in the manner

11 prescribed by David king of Israel; and they chanted praises and thanksgiving to the LORD, singing, 'It is good to give thanks to the LORD,*c* for his love towards Israel endures for ever.' All the people raised a great shout of praise to the LORD because the foundation of the house of

12 the LORD had been laid. But many of the priests and Levites and heads of families, who were old enough to have seen the former house, wept and wailed aloud when they saw the foundation of this house laid, while many

13 others shouted for joy at the top of their voice. The people could not distinguish the sound of the shout of joy

[a] Binnui, and Hodaviah: *prob. rdg.; Heb.* and his sons the family of Judah.

[b] *Prob. rdg.; Heb. adds* the family of Henadad, their family and their kinsmen the Levites.

[c] to give thanks to the LORD: *prob. rdg., cp. Ps. 106: 1; Heb. om.*

from that of the weeping and wailing, so great was the
shout which the people were raising, and the sound could
be heard a long way off.

✻ Having pictured the community eager to return to its
home, the Chronicler now pictures an immediate start on the
restoration of the temple. Curiously, however, nothing is here
heard of Sheshbazzar; instead the leaders of the community
are represented as Zerubbabel, a member of the Davidic
family, and Jeshua, the leading priest. This abrupt change certainly suggests that a different source of information is here
being used; it also raises the further question whether the
events here described really took place in 537 B.C. as is implied,
or whether Zerubbabel's leadership should not rather be
ascribed to a slightly later period. We have no certain knowledge, but the nature of the prophecies in Haggai and Zechariah, dated about 520 B.C., would be surprising if addressed to
those who had already been leaders of the community for
nearly two decades.

1. This verse also occurs at the conclusion of the parallel
version of the list (Neh. 7: 73*b* – 8: 1). It provides the occasion for a reference to the 'pilgrim-feast of Tabernacles' in
verse 4, which was observed in this month.

2. *Jeshua:* also found as 'Joshua', the form used in Haggai
and Zechariah. In Haggai (1: 1 and elsewhere) he is described
as 'high priest', the earliest historical use of this term. *Zerubbabel son of Shealtiel:* mentioned in 1 Chron. 3: 19, but there
described as one of the 'sons of Pedaiah'. Both Shealtiel and
Pedaiah were sons of the exiled king of Judah, Jehoiachin; it
is no longer possible to tell which tradition of Zerubbabel's
parentage is correct. His rule over the Jerusalem community
seems to be associated with the period of Darius I's early years,
about 520 B.C., and in Haggai he is the centre of great hopes of
restoration, but we know nothing of his subsequent history.
That is not to say, as has sometimes been suggested, that his

disappearance should be regarded as some kind of mystery that was occasioned by plots against the Persian rulers.

set to work and built the altar: the N.E.B. translation brings out the sense well. At the first opportunity the offering of sacrifice in accordance with the requirements of the Pentateuch is resumed. It is very unlikely that the site was in fact abandoned, as is here implied.

3. *fear of the foreign population:* a new theme is hinted at, which will be developed more fully in ch. 4, where further consideration will be given to the identity of this foreign population. We may simply note here that the translation is a rather free rendering of the Hebrew 'peoples of the lands'.

4–5. These verses picture the complete establishment of the sacrificial system, impractical as that may have been without the presence of any building.

6. *the foundation of the temple of the LORD had not yet been laid:* insofar as *foundation* in English suggests a completely new building, this translation may give a misleading impression. It is likely that the temple was ruinous, rather than completely demolished to the extent of needing new foundations.

8. *In the second year...in the second month:* the second year would be 537/6, but it is doubtful whether the activity here described took place so soon. Zerubbabel's career probably began later, and it is the Chronicler's concern to stress the immediacy of response which leads him to antedate this work. Again the reference to the second month may be an allusion to Solomon's work beginning at that time (2 Chron. 3: 2) – the substantial identity of the two temples is thereby stressed.

Levites from the age of twenty years: as throughout the Chronicler's work, the importance of the Levites' role is stressed. The age at which their service began varies according to different traditions; this agrees with 1 Chron. 23: 27, whereas other traditions refer to twenty-five or thirty years.

10. *the manner prescribed by David:* the theme of continuity appears again – what David had appointed for the first temple is once more inaugurated.

11. The N.E.B. translation has here gratuitously emended the Hebrew, as if this were a quotation of Ps. 106: 1 (see footnote). There is no need to suppose that an allusion is intended to any one particular Psalm known to us; the phrase is one frequently found in psalms.

12–13. This may be taken as an expression of conflicting natural emotions, but a different interpretation is also possible. There are many indications in the Bible and other ancient texts that weeping was not simply an expression of spontaneous emotion, but might have a formalized or ritual function, aimed at invoking the divine favour or pity. ✶

OPPOSITION

✶ A number of difficulties in the way of an historical reconstruction of the events in Ezra have already been noted, and in ch. 4 they become more acute. Several Persian emperors are mentioned – Cyrus, Darius, Ahasuerus, Artaxerxes (all in verses 5–7), and then Darius again in verse 24. The continuing context makes it clear that the Darius of verse 24 must be Darius I, emperor 522–486 B.C. The problem then arises as to the identification of Ahasuerus and Artaxerxes. Earlier attempts to identify them with rulers between Cyrus and Darius have now been abandoned, and it is generally agreed that the reference must be to the Ahasuerus and Artaxerxes who ruled in the fifth century B.C. In other words, what is preserved in this chapter is a record of various attempts to hinder the Jews of Jerusalem, with no chronological precision. Whether or not the Chronicler himself was aware of this chronological confusion is uncertain; but we can be confident that it would not be a matter of great concern to him – his purpose was to show the hand of God at work, guiding his people when they remained faithful to him, and bringing them through all difficulties to a restoration of true worship. With this in mind, we need not suppose that the various adversaries mentioned should be identified with one another;

the Chronicler was concerned not with the historical circumstances of the opposition, but with the way God's plans came to fruition. For all these reasons, though the chapter is here divided to help make historical sense of its material, it is also important to consider it as a whole. *

OPPOSITION IN THE REIGNS OF CYRUS AND DARIUS

4 When the enemies of Judah and Benjamin heard that the returned exiles were building a temple to the LORD
2 the God of Israel, they approached Zerubbabel and Jeshua[a] and the heads of families and said to them, 'Let us join you in building, for like you we seek your God, and we have been sacrificing to him ever[b] since the days of
3 Esarhaddon king of Assyria, who brought us here.' But Zerubbabel and Jeshua and the rest of the heads of families in Israel said to them, 'The house which we are building for our God is no concern of yours. We alone will build it for the LORD the God of Israel, as his majesty Cyrus king of Persia commanded us.'
4 Then the people of the land caused the Jews to lose
5 heart and made them afraid to continue building; and in order to defeat their purpose they bribed officials at court to act against them. This continued throughout the reign of Cyrus and into the reign of Darius king of Persia.

* 1. *the enemies of Judah and Benjamin:* as in 1: 5, the true community is described as *Judah and Benjamin*, rather than as 'Israel'. The identity of the enemies is very uncertain. In verse 2 they refer to their own ancestry as those who had been settled in the land by 'Esarhaddon king of Assyria'. This may

[a] and Jeshua: *prob. rdg., cp. 1 Esdras 5: 68; Heb. om.*
[b] and we...ever: *or, as otherwise read,* but we have not sacrificed.

26

simply be a comment by the Chronicler to stress their foreign
origins, but it is perfectly possible that an historical allusion is
contained here, and that a settlement had been made in the
former northern kingdom at the time of Esarhaddon (681–669
B.C.). Such settlers should not be confused with the Samaritans,
who were a conservative group within Judaism, associated
with the holy place on Mount Gerizim, near Shechem. There
is no clear reference to their existence before the very last
centuries B.C. The story that they were descended from
foreign settlers is a piece of later Jewish polemic, based on
2 Kings 17: 24–41.

2–3. The attitude of the groups here is important: the
enemies are anxious to help; the Jerusalem community firmly
rejects all such offers. Our sympathies naturally go to those
whose openness is rejected, but here as elsewhere the Chronicler is stressing that the Jerusalem community alone can be
responsible for the restoration of the holy place. Again, it is
difficult to decide what the original historical situation may
have been, and the problem here is rendered still more difficult
by the fact that the main Hebrew textual tradition has 'we
have not sacrificed' (see N.E.B. footnote), and this could be a
reference to the lack of any sacrifice during the time of exile,
or a deliberate note of disapproval by the Chronicler that the
foreign settlers had not maintained proper religious practice,
or simply a scribal error.

4–5. A further episode of opposition is now described,
which should probably be regarded as quite distinct from that
mentioned in verses 1–3. Here the adversaries are described as
the people of the land, and instead of the willingness to help
of those described in verse 2, the attitude of this group is one
of obstruction and hostility. Again, the identification of the
adversaries is a problem; they may be those who had continued
to live in Judah and resented interference from what to them
seemed like foreigners; or the term *people of the land* may
be used in its later sense of 'common people'. Again there is
no ground for any identification with the Samaritans. ✳

OPPOSITION IN THE REIGNS OF AHASUERUS
AND ARTAXERXES

6 At the beginning of the reign of Ahasuerus, the people of the land brought a charge in writing against the inhabitants of Judah and Jerusalem.

7 And in the days of Artaxerxes king of Persia, with the agreement of Mithredath, Tabeel and all his colleagues wrote to him; the letter was written in Aramaic and read aloud in Aramaic.

8[a] Rehum the high commissioner and Shimshai the secretary wrote a letter to King Artaxerxes concerning Jerusalem in the following terms:

9 From Rehum the high commissioner, Shimshai the secretary, and all their colleagues, the judges, the commissioners, the overseers, and chief officers, the men o

10 Erech and Babylon, and the Elamites in Susa, and the other peoples whom the great and renowned Asnappar[b] deported and settled in the city of Samaria and in the rest of the province of Beyond-Euphrates.

11 Here follows the text of their letter:

To King Artaxerxes from his servants, the men of the province of Beyond-Euphrates:

12 Be it known to Your Majesty that the Jews who left you and came to these parts have reached Jerusalem and are rebuilding that wicked and rebellious city; they have surveyed[c] the foundations and are completing[d]

[a] *From 4: 8 to 6: 18 the text is in Aramaic.* [b] *Or* Osnappar.
[c] have surveyed: *prob. rdg.; Aram.* are surveying.
[d] are completing: *so Vulg.; Aram.* have completed.

the walls. Be it known to Your Majesty that, if their 13
city is rebuilt and the walls are completed, they will pay
neither general levy, nor poll-tax, nor land-tax, and in
the end[a] they will harm the monarchy. Now, because 14
we eat the king's salt and it is not right that we should
witness the king's dishonour, therefore we have sent to
inform Your Majesty, in order that search may be 15
made in the annals of your predecessors. You will discover by searching through the annals that this has
been a rebellious city, harmful to the monarchy and its
provinces, and that sedition has long been rife within
its walls. That is why the city was laid waste. We sub- 16
mit to Your Majesty that, if it is rebuilt and its walls are
completed, the result will be that you will have no more
footing in the province of Beyond-Euphrates.

The king sent this answer: 17

To Rehum the high commissioner, Shimshai the
secretary, and all your colleagues resident in Samaria
and in the rest of the province of Beyond-Euphrates,
greeting. The letter which you sent to me has now been 18
read clearly in my presence. I have given orders and 19
search has been made, and it has been found that the
city in question has a long history of revolt against the
monarchy, and that rebellion and sedition have been
rife in it. Powerful kings have ruled in Jerusalem, 20
exercising authority over the whole province of
Beyond-Euphrates, and general levy, poll-tax, and
land-tax have been paid to them. Therefore, issue 21
orders that these men must desist. This city is not to be

[a] in the end: *or* certainly.

22 rebuilt until a decree to that effect is issued by me. See that you do not neglect your duty in this matter, lest more damage and harm be done to the monarchy.

23 When the text of the letter from King Artaxerxes was read before Rehum the high commissioner,[a] Shimshai the secretary, and their colleagues, they hurried to Jerusalem and forcibly compelled the Jews to stop work.

✻ 6. *Ahasuerus:* perhaps better known in English as Xerxes, a form of his name derived from Greek. He was king of Persia 486–465 B.C., and is best known for his unsuccessful attempt to conquer Greece. He plays little part in the biblical record, the most important reference being in the book of Esther where he is represented (probably unhistorically) as having a Jewish wife, Esther. This isolated verse seems to be included only because it provides a further allusion to opposition. Its nature is unknown – the reference to *the people of the land* has been supplied by N.E.B. to make the translation smoother and is not in the Hebrew.

7. A further occasion of opposition, again with no detail of the circumstances, save that we have now reached the reign of Artaxerxes (presumably Artaxerxes I, 465–424 B.C.). It appears that the Chronicler is here simply drawing together all the traditions concerning opposition that were available to him, to show how much the community's loyalty was tested. The absence of more detailed information may not have been a matter of great concern to him.

with the agreement of: the older English versions follow the Hebrew in taking this to be another name, 'Bishlam'; the emendation made by the N.E.B. is a minor and probable one, though it is not indicated in a footnote.

in Aramaic: Aramaic, a language closely akin to Hebrew, was used for international correspondence within the Persian

[a] the high commissioner: *so Pesh.; Aram. om.*

Empire. The purpose of the note here appears to be a kind of scribal warning that the next section is to be in that language. The Aramaic section which begins here continues to 6: 18.

8. The last occasion of opposition is dealt with more fully; like the preceding one, it is set in the time of Artaxerxes, though as far as we can tell the two incidents are unrelated.

9–10. The officials listed here appear to be Persian governmental officers in the province of *Beyond-Euphrates* which included Judah. We have no knowledge based directly on Persian sources, but from Greek writers it appears that the Persian Empire was divided into twenty provinces known as satrapies, of which Beyond-Euphrates (that is, 'beyond' from the Persian point of view) will have been one. It may have been based on Damascus, or possibly Samaria, since for the most part the Persians maintained the administrative system set up by the Assyrians some 200 years earlier. The idea of continuity here expressed is thus entirely credible. Again, there is no link with the Samaritans save in later Jewish attacks; their home was not Samaria but Shechem.

10. *Asnappar:* the name, unknown as such, is probably a corruption of the last great Assyrian king Assurbanipal (669–633 B.C.), but the tradition preserved by the Jewish historian Josephus mentions 'Shalmaneser', an earlier Assyrian king. In any case both this verse and verse 2 appear to point to a tradition of a series of Assyrian deportations into the territory of Israel.

12–13. The nature of the complaint is different from that alluded to in the earlier part of the chapter. Here, more political opposition is involved; the complainants are afraid that Jerusalem will regain its former independent position and no longer be loyal to the Persian rulers. Whether the letter was motivated by genuine concern or by jealousy is impossible to tell; the Chronicler clearly sees it as illustrative of the obstacles in the way of the community, which may once indeed have been 'a rebellious city' (verse 15); but is now loyal both to its God and to the imperial authorities.

31

It is noteworthy that both the complaint and the royal reply make no reference to the temple, but are concerned with rebuilding the city and its walls. This was a major concern of Nehemiah, and its mention here should serve to remind us that there is much in the detailed history of Jerusalem of which we know nothing.

20. *Powerful kings:* if the letter is a genuine fragment from the royal archives, this would be part of a universal tendency to exaggerate the power of one's enemies. Equally, it may be the Chronicler's way of referring obliquely to David's greatness.

These varied fragments of material, largely from the fifth century B.C., and dealing with the city as a whole, are now used by the Chronicler as illustrative of a sixth-century situation relating to the temple. The history is chaotic; the unity of theme impressive. ✶

CAN THE TEMPLE BE REBUILT?

24 From then onwards the work on the house of God in Jerusalem stopped; and it remained at a standstill till the second year of the reign of Darius king of Persia.

5 But the prophets Haggai[a] and Zechariah grandson[b] of Iddo upbraided the Jews in Judah and Jerusalem, pro-
2 phesying in the name of the God of Israel. Then Zerubbabel son of Shealtiel and Jeshua son of Jozadak at once began to rebuild the house of God in Jerusalem, and the prophets of God were with them and supported them.
3 Tattenai, governor of the province of Beyond-Euphrates, Shethar-bozenai, and their colleagues promptly came to them and said, 'Who issued a decree permitting you to
4 rebuild this house and complete its furnishings?' They[c]

[a] Prob. rdg., cp. 1 Esdras 6: 1; Aram. adds the prophet.
[b] Lit. son.   [c] So Pesh.; Aram. We.

32

also asked them for the names of the men engaged in the building. But the elders of the Jews were under God's 5 watchful eye, and they were not prevented from continuing the work, until such time as a report should reach Darius and a royal letter should be received in answer.

Here follows the text of the letter sent by Tattenai, 6 govenor of the province of Beyond-Euphrates, Shethar-bozenai, and his colleagues, the inspectors in the province of Beyond-Euphrates, to King Darius. This is the written 7 report that they sent:

To King Darius, all greetings. Be it known to Your 8 Majesty that we went to the province of Judah and found the house of the great God being rebuilt by the Jewish elders,*a* with massive stones and timbers laid in the walls. The work was being done thoroughly and was making good progress under their direction. We 9 asked these elders who had issued a decree for the rebuilding of this house and the completion of the furnishings. We also asked them for their names, so 10 that we might make a list of the leaders for your information. This was their reply: 'We are the servants 11 of the God of heaven and earth, and we are rebuilding the house originally built many years ago; a great king of Israel built it and completed it. But because our fore- 12 fathers provoked the anger of the God of heaven, he put them into the power of Nebuchadnezzar the Chaldaean, king of Babylon, who pulled down this house and carried the people captive to Babylon. However, 13 Cyrus king of Babylon in the first year of his reign

[a] by...elders: *prob. rdg., cp.* 1 Esdras 6: 8; *Aram. om.*

issued a decree that this house of God should be rebuilt.
14 Moreover, there were gold and silver vessels of the house of God, which Nebuchadnezzar had taken from the temple in Jerusalem and put in the temple in Babylon; and these King Cyrus took out of the temple in Babylon. He gave them to a man named Shesh-
15 bazzar, whom he had appointed governor, and said to him, "Take these vessels; go and restore them to the temple in Jerusalem, and let the house of God there be
16 rebuilt on its original site." Then this Sheshbazzar came and laid the foundation of the house of God in Jerusalem; and from that time until now the rebuilding has
17 continued, but it is not yet finished.' Now, therefore, if it please Your Majesty, let search be made in the royal archives in Babylon, to discover whether a decree was issued by King Cyrus for the rebuilding of this house of God in Jerusalem. Then let the king send us his wishes in the matter.

✳ To appreciate the force of this section it is necessary to set aside our historical knowledge that the correspondence in ch. 4 is in fact of later date than the events here recorded. Probably the Chronicler himself, and certainly his earliest readers, will not have been aware of this. To them, the picture was of a rebuff from the imperial authorities; could further search lead to a restoration of favour? Woven into this dramatic story is a reference to the prophetic activity of Haggai and Zechariah, as an indication that God was at work guiding his people and providing the necessary encouragement for the leaders.

5:1. *Haggai and Zechariah:* these prophets were active around 520 B.C., at the beginning of the reign of Darius, and each of

them had as a major concern the place of the temple as showing God's presence with his people. It may well be that their
prophecies (in the books of Haggai and Zechariah 1–8, the
remaining chapters not being from Zechariah) were edited by
someone of the Chronicler's circle. *grandson of Iddo:* the
N.E.B. has modified the usual meaning of the Aramaic text to
agree with Zech. 1: 1 (see footnote), but it is also possible that
'son of Iddo' is correct and the reference to 'Berechiah' in
Zech 1: 1 is mistaken.

1–2. These verses in effect supply a summary of the message
of the two prophets, prophetic warnings leading to renewed
activity and consequent prophetic support.

3. *Tattenai:* he is identified as the provincial *governor* – the
word used is that which Hag. 1: 1 applies to Zerubbabel, but
Tattenai will have occupied a more important position, and
may be referred to in tablets from this period which have been
discovered. The action he takes does not imply hostility but a
concern to be kept fully informed of what was going on in the
province under his responsibility.

5. *they were not prevented from continuing the work:* the
benevolence of the royal officials is indicated, and the purely
precautionary nature of Tattenai's enquiry suggested.

8. *the great God:* however friendly disposed were the royal
officials, this is still unexpected language. Quite possibly the
Chronicler is paraphrasing the letter rather than setting down
a word-for-word transcription.

11–12. These verses provide an admirable summary of the
period of the divided monarchy as the Chronicler himself
interpreted them.

14. The Chronicler's interests are again seen in the stress on
the vessels, and the reference to Sheshbazzar links back to ch. 1.

16. *Sheshbazzar* is here credited with laying *the foundation
of the house of God*, whereas according to ch. 3 this had been
done under the leadership of Zerubbabel. We have already
seen (p. 4) that this Aramaic story seems to be a parallel to
the Hebrew story in chs. 1–3 and here, as elsewhere, the

35

Chronicler may have set down parallel accounts of the same events without attempting to harmonize them. ✳

6 Then King Darius issued an order, and search was made in the archives where the treasures were deposited in
2 Babylon. But it was in Ecbatana, in the royal residence in the province of Media, that a scroll was found, on which was written the following memorandum:

3   In the first year of King Cyrus, the king issued this decree concerning the house of God in Jerusalem: Let the house be rebuilt as a place where sacrifices are offered and fire-offerings brought. Its height shall be
4 sixty cubits and its breadth sixty cubits, with three courses of massive stones and one[a] course of timber, the
5 cost to be defrayed from the royal treasury. Also the gold and silver vessels of the house of God, which Nebuchadnezzar took out of the temple in Jerusalem and brought to Babylon, shall be restored; they shall all be taken back to the temple in Jerusalem, and restored each to its place in the house of God.

6 Then King Darius issued this order:[b]

      Now, Tattenai, governor of the province of Beyond-Euphrates, Shethar-bozenai, and your colleagues, the inspectors in the province of Beyond-Euphrates, you
7 are to keep away from the place, and to leave the governor of the Jews and their elders free to rebuild

[a] *Prob. rdg., cp. 1 Esdras 6: 25; Aram.* a new.
[b] *Then...order: prob. rdg., cp. 1 Esdras 6: 27; Aram. om.*

this house of God; let them rebuild it on its original site. I also issue an order prescribing what you are to do 8 for these elders of the Jews, so that the said house of God may be rebuilt. Their expenses are to be defrayed in full from the royal funds accruing from the taxes of the province of Beyond-Euphrates, so that the work may not be brought to a standstill. And let them have 9 daily without fail whatever they want, young bulls, rams, or lambs as whole-offerings for the God of heaven, or wheat, salt, wine, or oil, as the priests in Jerusalem demand, so that they may offer soothing 10 sacrifices to the God of heaven, and pray for the life of the king and his sons. Furthermore, I decree that, if any 11 man tampers with this edict, a beam shall be pulled out of his house and he shall be fastened erect to it and flogged; and, in addition, his house shall be forfeit.[a] And may the God who made that place a dwelling for 12 his Name overthrow any king or people that shall presume to tamper with this edict or to destroy this house of God in Jerusalem. I Darius have issued a decree; it is to be carried out to the letter.

Then Tattenai, governor of the province of Beyond- 13 Euphrates, Shethar-bozenai, and their colleagues carried out to the letter the instructions which King Darius had sent them, and the elders of the Jews went on with the 14 rebuilding. As a result of the prophecies of Haggai the prophet and Zechariah grandson[b] of Iddo they had good success and finished the rebuilding as commanded by the God of Israel and according to the decrees of Cyrus and

[a] Or made into a dunghill (*mng. of Aram. word uncertain*).
[b] *Lit.* son.

15 Darius;[a] and the house was completed on the twenty-third[b] day of the month Adar, in the sixth year of King Darius.

16 Then the people of Israel, the priests and the Levites and all the other exiles who had returned, celebrated the
17 dedication of the house of God with great rejoicing. For its dedication they offered one hundred bulls, two hundred rams, and four hundred lambs, and as a sin-offering for all Israel twelve he-goats, corresponding to the num-
18 ber of the tribes of Israel. And they re-established the priests in their groups and the Levites in their divisions for the service of God in Jerusalem, as prescribed in the book of Moses.

19 On the fourteenth day of the first month the exiles who
20 had returned kept the Passover. The priests and the Levites, one and all, had purified themselves; all of them were ritually clean, and they killed the passover lamb for all the exiles who had returned, for their fellow-priests
21 and for themselves. It was eaten by the Israelites who had come back from exile and by all who had separated themselves from the peoples of the land and their uncleanness
22 and sought the LORD the God of Israel. And they kept the pilgrim-feast of Unleavened Bread for seven days with rejoicing; for the LORD had given them cause for joy by changing the disposition of the king of Assyria towards them, so that he encouraged them in the work of the house of God, the God of Israel.

✳ This chapter is a direct continuation of the preceding one, and tells of the happy conclusion of the investigation started by

[a] *Prob. rdg.; Aram. adds* and Artaxerxes king of Persia.
[b] *Prob. rdg., cp.* 1 *Esdras* 7: 5; *Aram.* third.

Tattenai, and of the completion of the building of the temple. This is presented as the first great climax in the life of the community newly returned from its exile in Babylon.

2. *in Ecbatana:* this was far away to the east, *in the province of Media*, in the heart of modern Iran. The Persian kings lived in different parts of their empire at different times of the year, and this was the summer capital. A detail such as this, which apparently has no theological significance, strongly suggests that here the Chronicler is drawing upon reliable sources of historical information.

3–5. The form of the decree here reproduced differs in two main ways from that found in ch. 1. It is in Aramaic rather than Hebrew, and it concentrates on restoration of the temple, in accordance with Persian policy known from other parts of the empire, without referring to the return of exiles. For both these reasons, it is likely that we are here much closer to the original form of edict, though this is less certain in the case of the reference to *the gold and silver vessels*.

6. *Then King Darius issued this order:* there is nothing corresponding to this phrase in the Aramaic text, and the reference to 1 Esdras 6: 27 in the N.E.B. footnote is not very relevant. In the original, the instructions to Tattenai follow immediately upon the decree.

9. It was regular Persian practice to subsidize local forms of worship; whether these subsidies could be virtually 'on demand', as is here implied, is more doubtful.

11. Such a threat of punishment in the event of non-compliance is a regular feature of documents of this kind in the ancient world – and indeed of the modern, though usually in less picturesque language.

12. Also characteristic of Persian custom was to invoke the favour of the gods of subject peoples.

14. The successful completion of the work is here ascribed to two causes, both very important for the Chronicler: the favour of the Persian authorities and the work of the prophets.

The reference to 'Artaxerxes king of Persia' (see N.E.B.

footnote) in the Aramaic text reminds us that the Chronicler's main concern is to present the policy of all the Persian rulers as consistently doing justice to Israel. Artaxerxes did not in fact rule until the next century, and we cannot be certain whether or not the Chronicler was himself aware of this chronological confusion.

15. The date of the completion is subject to some uncertainty, as the N.E.B. footnote shows. The year – *the sixth... of King Darius* – was 515 B.C., and the month *Adar*, the last in the year, that is to say, our March. The actual day is problematic: the Aramaic text has 'third', but other ancient traditions have *twenty-third*, which the N.E.B. translators have preferred. This may be right, though the change could also be due to the desire to have the completion of the temple-building come just at the end of the year, so that the rededicated building would be ready for the new year. Some doubt has been cast on this date because of its suspicious closeness to an exact seventy-year period since the temple's destruction by Nebuchadnezzar, but there is no attempt to make the period precisely seventy years, or to call attention to the coincidence, and it seems best to accept the information given here as reliable.

16–18. These verses describe *the dedication of the house of God*. An instructive comparison can be made with 2 Chron. 7, describing the dedication of Solomon's temple; though similar phraseology is used, everything is now on a much smaller scale. This is one of the strata which speak in terms of all *the tribes of Israel*, as against other sections which speak of 'Judah and Benjamin' only. Some of the differences may be explicable in terms of the context, but others run deeper and suggest significantly different traditions.

At this point the Aramaic section ends and Hebrew is resumed, with a section which in many ways reads like a conclusion of the ceremony described in ch. 3.

19. *the exiles who had returned kept the Passover*: stress is laid upon the fact that the true community consisted of those who

had been in exile, whose troubles were now in a sense over, though the work of restoration is not yet complete. The reference to Passover is an important indication that in the later Old Testament period this Spring festival assumed the importance that had formerly been associated with the Autumn festival, Tabernacles. But it is also important to bear in mind that on two previous occasions in the history of the people, under kings Hezekiah and Josiah, the culminating event was described as a celebration of Passover (2 Chron. 30 and 35), and the present ceremony is clearly comparable with these earlier ones.

21. *and by all who had separated themselves from the peoples of the land:* the festival was open to other Israelites who were willing to commit themselves fully to the newly established community, and this welcome is important when we consider the policy of Ezra and his attitude to those outside the community. We cannot precisely identify those who *had separated themselves*, any more than those addressed in the comparable celebration under Hezekiah (2 Chron. 30: 6–9), but we may regard this as at least in part an invitation directed at those who had fallen away from the Jerusalem community, or were liable to do so, in the Chronicler's own day. The phrase *peoples of the land* is reminiscent of that used in 4: 4.

22. *the king of Assyria:* this is hardly a simple mistake for 'Persia', which seems the clear meaning, but it is difficult to know what exactly caused this expression. There is no other indication in the Chronicler of the use of *Assyria* as a general term for the heathen empire as its capital Nineveh seems to be used for a typical heathen capital in the story of Jonah. ✶

Ezra's mission to Jerusalem

EZRA THE SCRIBE

7 NOW AFTER THESE EVENTS, in the reign of Artaxerxes
king of Persia, there came up from Babylon one Ezra
2 son of Seraiah, son of Azariah, son of Hilkiah, son of
3 Shallum, son of Zadok, son[a] of Ahitub, son of Amariah,
4 son of Azariah, son of Meraioth, son of Zerahiah, son of
5 Uzzi, son of Bukki, son of Abishua, son of Phinehas, son
6 of Eleazar, son of Aaron the chief priest. He was a scribe[b]
learned in the law of Moses which the LORD the God of
Israel had given them; and the king granted him all that
he asked, for the hand of the LORD his God was upon
7 him. In the seventh year of King Artaxerxes, other
Israelites, priests, Levites, singers, door-keepers, and
8 temple-servitors went up with him to Jerusalem; and
they reached Jerusalem in the fifth month, in the seventh
9 year of the king. On the first day of the first month Ezra
fixed the day for departure from Babylon, and on the
first day of the fifth month he arrived at Jerusalem, for the
10 gracious hand of his God was upon him. For Ezra had
devoted himself to the study and observance of the law
of the LORD and to teaching statute and ordinance in Israel.

* The restoration of the temple was clearly a major climax
for the Chronicler; now he passes without any mention of
what must have been a long intervening period to the work of
Ezra himself. His achievement is clearly regarded as setting the

[a] *Or* grandson.　　　[b] *Or* doctor of the law.

seal on the work of restoration, and long after his lifetime he was venerated among at least some groups within Judaism as the one who had done more than anyone since the time of Moses to give Judaism its distinctive character. To him came to be ascribed the gathering of the sacred books which form the Hebrew Bible; the use of the Aramaic script, still used in writing Hebrew today, instead of the archaic Hebrew script, was attributed to him, and an extensive collection of apocryphal literature gathered around his name. Conversely, for those who came later to separate from the Judaism of Jerusalem, such as the Samaritans, he was the object of bitter condemnation.

It is difficult to be confident about the original role of Ezra. Some scholars have regarded him as no more than a figment of the Chronicler's imagination, but we need scarcely doubt his existence. Nevertheless, great uncertainty remains on two questions in particular. We cannot be sure whether he should be dated under Artaxerxes I or II, that is, in 458 or 398 B.C. (see pp. 6–8), and we cannot establish the nature of his original mission. Later tradition regarded his role as essentially religious, but it is possible that originally he had a task to perform similar to that of Nehemiah, of a political nature, to maintain the loyalty and peace of Judah on behalf of the Persian government, for whom this was a sensitive area on the border with Egypt.

But if that was the origin of his work, it has largely been overlaid in the present account, which concentrates on two aspects of his accomplishment – the purification of the religious community in Jerusalem, which is the concern of the remainder of the book of Ezra, and the reading of the law, which is described in Neh. 8. These opening verses provide the setting.

1. *Now after these events:* we know that a gap either of sixty years or of more than a century is involved here; for the Chronicler, the whole was a unity, one action by God on behalf of his people. The references to *Artaxerxes* in chs. 4 and

6 (see N.E.B. footnote to 6: 14) will have helped to establish this unity. *from Babylon:* Ezra is established as having undergone the experience of exile appropriate for the true community. *Ezra son of Seraiah: son of* here might mean 'descendant of', but it is also possible that the Chronicler is presenting Ezra as the son of the priest who was sent into exile (2 Kings 25: 18), to establish more firmly Ezra's links with the exiles. Again our knowledge of the impossibility of the chronology may be a hindrance to our grasp of the author's intention.

1–5. The genealogy which follows is parallel to that found, either as a whole or in part, at several places in the Chronicler's work: 1 Chron. 6: 3–15 and 50–3; 1 Chron. 9: 11; and Neh. 11: 11. We should be cautious about treating this as a genuine family-tree; it appears to be a recognized priestly genealogy, to which the name of Ezra – found only in this form of the list – was added. The importance of establishing an appropriate genealogy has already been made clear by the account in 2: 59–63 of those unable to do so.

6. *a scribe learned in the law of Moses:* the significance of this description of Ezra is not certain. The word translated *scribe* can mean a high-ranking political official, and later in the chapter this is the impression of Ezra's position that is conveyed. But *scribe* also came to mean one learned in the scriptures (in the New Testament sense of 'scribes and Pharisees') and the qualifying phrase here suggests that that was how the Chronicler meant us to understand Ezra's work. *the king granted him all that he asked:* this is the first of a number of points at which very close parallels will become apparent between the mission of Ezra and that of Nehemiah, who also was given authority by the Persian king in response to his own request (Neh. 2: 4–10).

7. *In the seventh year of King Artaxerxes:* the Chronicler clearly envisages this as being the same Artaxerxes as has already been mentioned. But his lack of knowledge of, or concern for, details of Persian history make it perfectly possible that the reference could be to Artaxerxes II. The date

could thus be 458 or 398 B.C. Either of these alternatives seems preferable to the suggestion sometimes made that *seventh* is an error for some other figure. *other Israelites...temple-servitors:* the classes listed in ch. 2 are here summarized, and the impression is created of a solemn religious procession returning to the holy city. *

EZRA'S COMMISSION

This is a copy of the royal letter which King Arta- 11 xerxes had given to Ezra the priest and scribe, a scribe versed in questions concerning the commandments and the statutes of the LORD laid upon Israel:

Artaxerxes, king of kings, to Ezra the priest and 12[a] scribe learned in the law of the God of heaven:

This is my decision. I hereby issue a decree that any 13 of the people of Israel or of its priests or Levites in my kingdom who volunteer to go to Jerusalem may go with you. You are sent by the king and his seven 14 counsellors to find out how things stand in Judah and Jerusalem with regard to the law of your God with which you are entrusted. You are also to convey the 15 silver and gold which the king and his counsellors have freely offered to the God of Israel whose dwelling is in Jerusalem, together with any silver and gold that you 16 may find throughout the province of Babylon, and the voluntary offerings of the people and of the priests which they freely offer for the house of their God in Jerusalem. In pursuance of this decree you shall use the 17 money solely for the purchase of bulls, rams, and lambs, and the proper grain-offerings and drink-

[a] *The text of verses 12–26 is in Aramaic.*

offerings, to be offered on the altar in the house of your
18 God in Jerusalem. Further, should any silver and gold
be left over, you and your colleagues may use it at your
19 discretion according to the will of your God. The
vessels which have been given you for the service of the
house of your God you shall hand over to the God of
20 Jerusalem; and if anything else should be required for
the house of your God, which it may fall to you to
provide, you may provide it out of the king's treasury.

21 And I, King Artaxerxes, issue an order to all treasur-
ers in the province of Beyond-Euphrates that whatever
is demanded of you by Ezra the priest, a scribe learned
in the law of the God of heaven, is to be supplied
22 exactly, up to a hundred talents of silver, a hundred kor
of wheat, a hundred bath of wine, a hundred bath of
23 oil, and salt without reckoning. Whatever is demanded
by the God of heaven, let it be diligently carried out for
the house of the God of heaven; otherwise wrath may
24 fall upon the realm of the king and his sons. We also
make known to you that you have no authority to
impose general levy, poll-tax, or land-tax on any of the
priests, Levites, musicians, door-keepers, temple-
servitors, or other servants of this house of God.

25 And you, Ezra, in accordance with the wisdom of
your God with which you are entrusted, are to appoint
arbitrators and judges to judge all your people in the
province of Beyond-Euphrates, all who acknowledge
the laws of your God;[a] and you and they are to instruct
26 those who do not acknowledge them. Whoever will

[a] to judge...your God: *or* all of them versed in the laws of your God,
to judge all the people in the province of Beyond-Euphrates.

not obey the law of your God and the law of the king, let
judgement be rigorously executed upon him, be it death,
banishment, confiscation of property, or imprisonment.

Then Ezra said,[a] 'Blessed be the LORD the God of our 27
fathers who has prompted the king thus to add glory to
the house of the LORD in Jerusalem, and has made the 28
king and his counsellors and all his high officers well disposed towards me!'

So, knowing that the hand of the LORD my God was
upon me, I took courage and assembled leading men out
of Israel to go up with me.

* After the summary picture of Ezra's work there now follows another Aramaic document (verses 12–26) setting out
more fully Ezra's task and the authorization he received from
the Persian rulers. As with the other Aramaic material in the
book, there is a likelihood that we have access here to official
documents, though we should not exclude the possibility that
they have been worked over by the Chronicler in the light of
his own point of view.

11. *priest and scribe:* these two descriptions of Ezra have been
established in the opening verses, *priest* by the genealogy,
scribe by the description in verse 6.

12. *learned in the law of the God of heaven:* this might be an
amplification of the description already given, but can also be
understood as a Persian title. *the God of heaven* appears to
have been a Persian mode of describing Yahweh and this title
would then make Ezra something like a 'commissioner for
Jewish affairs'.

13–20. The royal decree here brings out another parallel
with the Nehemiah narrative. The exemptions there described
in summary form (Neh. 2: 7–9) are here spelt out in more

[a] Then Ezra said: *prob. rdg., cp. 1 Esdras 8: 25; Heb. om.*

47

detail, and with greater emphasis on religious requisites.
There is also a marked similarity with the orders of Darius in
6: 6–12. It is difficult to know how far this similarity is due to
similar origin in the official style of Persian decrees, or whether
the hand of the Chronicler should be seen in each case.

16. *any silver and gold that you may find throughout the province
of Babylon:* here at least it seems certain that some secondary
idealization has taken place.

21. Again there appears to be an element of exaggeration;
the quantities listed here are very large indeed, for what seems
to have been quite a small-scale operation.

25. *arbitrators and judges:* this would be understood by the
Chronicler's readers as a religious reference, but if it formed
part of the original decree, it may well have had a more
political implication – part of Ezra's commission was to ensure
the stability of the area by the appointment of appropriate
local officials. Whether such appointments were in fact made
is not indicated by the traditions that have survived.

27–8. These verses are in Hebrew, and they also mark a
shift from the third-person description of Ezra found so far to
a first-person account. The prayer of thanksgiving, in a
frequently-found form, is used to punctuate the narrative in a
way similar to the use of interjected prayers in the Nehemiah
story. Similar also is the repeated confidence in the divine
guidance: *knowing that the hand of the LORD my God was
upon me.* ✻

EZRA'S JOURNEY TO JERUSALEM

8 These are the heads of families, as registered, family by
family, of those who went up with me from Babylon in
2 the reign of King Artaxerxes: of the family of Phinehas,
Gershom; of the family of Ithamar, Daniel; of the family
3 of David, Hattush son of[a] Shecaniah; of the family of

[a] son of: *prob. rdg.; Heb.* of the family of.

Parosh, Zechariah, and with him a hundred and fifty
males in the register; of the family of Pahath-moab, 4
Elihoenai son of Zerahiah, and with him two hundred
males; of the family of Zattu,[a] Shecaniah son of Jahaziel, 5
and with him three hundred males; of the family of Adin, 6
Ebed son of Jonathan, and with him fifty males; of the 7
family of Elam, Isaiah son of Athaliah, and with him
seventy males; of the family of Shephatiah, Zebadiah son 8
of Michael, and with him eighty males; of the family of 9
Joab, Obadiah son of Jehiel, and with him two hundred
and eighteen males; of the family of Bani,[b] Shelomith son 10
of Josiphiah, and with him a hundred and sixty males; of 11
the family of Bebai, Zechariah son of Bebai, and with him
twenty-eight males; of the family of Azgad, Johanan son 12
of Hakkatan, and with him a hundred and ten males. The 13
last were the family of Adonikam, and these were their
names: Eliphelet, Jeiel, and Shemaiah, and with them
sixty males; and the family of Bigvai, Uthai and Zabbud, 14
and with them seventy males.

I assembled them by the river which flows toward 15
Ahava; and we encamped there three days. When I
reviewed the people and the priests, I found no Levite
there. So I sent Eliezer, Ariel, Shemaiah, Elnathan, Jarib, 16
Elnathan, Nathan, Zechariah, and Meshullam, prominent
men, and Joiarib and Elnathan, men of discretion, with 17
instructions to go to Iddo, the chief man of the settlement
at Casiphia; and I gave them a message for him and[c] his
kinsmen, the temple-servitors there, asking for servitors
for the house of our God to be sent to us. And, because 18

[a] of Zattu: *prob. rdg., cp. 1 Esdras 8: 32; Heb. om.*　　　[b] of Bani:
prob. rdg., cp. 1 Esdras 8: 36; Heb. om.　　[c] and: *so Vulg.; Heb. om.*

the gracious hand of our God was upon us, they let us
have Sherebiah, a man of discretion, of the family of
Mahli son of Levi, son of Israel, together with his sons
19 and kinsmen, eighteen men; also Hashabiah, together
with Isaiah of the family of Merari, his kinsmen and their
20 sons, twenty men; besides two hundred and twenty
temple-servitors (this was an order instituted by David
and his officers to assist the Levites). These were all
indicated by name.

21   Then I proclaimed a fast there by the river Ahava, so
that we might mortify ourselves before our God and ask
from him a safe journey for ourselves, our dependants,
22 and all our possessions. For I was ashamed to ask the king
for an escort of soldiers and horsemen to help us against
enemies on the way, because we had said to the king,
'The hand of our God is upon all who seek him, working
their good; but his fierce anger is on all who forsake him.'
23 So we fasted and asked our God for a safe journey, and he
answered our prayer.

24   Then I separated twelve of the chiefs of the priests,
together with*a* Sherebiah and Hashabiah and ten of their
25 kinsmen, and handed over to them the silver and gold
and the vessels which had been set aside by the king, his
counsellors and his officers and all the Israelites who were
26 present, as their contribution to the house of our God. I
handed over to them six hundred and fifty talents of
silver, a hundred silver vessels weighing two talents, a
27 hundred talents of gold, twenty golden bowls worth a
thousand drachmas, and two vessels of a fine red copper,*b*

[a] together with: *prob. rdg.*, *cp. 1 Esdras 8: 54; Heb. om.*
[b] red copper: *or* orichalc.

precious as gold. And I said to the men, 'You are dedica- 28
ted to the LORD, and the vessels too are sacred; the silver
and gold are a voluntary offering to the LORD the God of
your fathers. Watch over them and guard them, until you 29
hand them over in the presence of the chiefs of the priests
and the Levites and the heads of families of Israel in
Jerusalem, in the rooms of the house of the LORD.'

So the priests and Levites received the consignment of 30
silver and gold and vessels, to be taken to the house of our
God in Jerusalem; and on the twelfth day of the first 31
month we left the river Ahava bound for Jerusalem. The
hand of our God was upon us, and he saved us from
enemy attack and from ambush on the way. When we 32
arrived at Jerusalem, we rested for three days. And on the 33
fourth day the silver and gold and the vessels were
deposited in the house of our God in the charge of Meremoth son of Uriah the priest, who had with him Eleazar
son of Phinehas, and they had with them the Levites
Jozabad son of Jeshua and Noadiah son of Binnui. Every- 34
thing was checked as it was handed over, and at the same
time a written record was made of the whole consignment. Then those who had come home from captivity, 35
the exiles who had returned, offered as whole-offerings
to the God of Israel twelve bulls for all Israel, ninety-six
rams and seventy-two[a] lambs, with twelve he-goats as a
sin-offering; all these were offered as a whole-offering to
the LORD. They also delivered the king's commission to 36
the royal satraps and governors in the province of
Beyond-Euphrates; and these gave support to the people
and the house of God.

[a] *Prob. rdg., cp. 1 Esdras 8: 65; Heb.* seventy-seven.

✻ What was described in summary form at the beginning of ch. 7 is now set out more fully in a first-person narrative which may represent an Ezra-source, though we should not necessarily regard it as reaching its present form at the hand of Ezra himself. At least the Chronicler's work is to be seen in the characteristic list of names which begins the account.

2. *of the family of David, Hattush:* there are few references to members of the Davidic line, apart from Zerubbabel, and Hattush, inserted after the priestly leaders, is not to play any significant part in the story. The N.E.B. emendation may be correct, but it is somewhat greater than is implied in the footnote, for the Hebrew text has: 'of the family of Hattush; [verse 3] of the family of Shecaniah' (where a name would then seem to be missing). We should not necessarily assume that Shecaniah was the father of Hattush, since a similar ambiguity occurs at the other points where these names are listed (1 Chron. 3: 22).

3–14. The twelve families listed here all appear – sometimes in the same order – in the list in 2: 3–15, of which it is clear that this is a variant form.

15. *the river which flows toward Ahava:* the site is unknown. Most probably it was one of the Babylonian irrigation canals, comparable to the 'river Kebar' of Ezek. 1: 1. *I found no Levite there:* the criticism which seems to be implied here is one of the few occasions in the work of the Chronicler where the Levites are not unreservedly praised, though the importance of the Levites is also stressed – the mission cannot take place without them.

16. What at first glance looks like a press-gang party is in reality quite different. These men – none of whom are mentioned in the preceding list – make up a kind of liturgical procession which in due course returns with an important part of the preparation, the gathering of the right personnel, accomplished.

17. *the settlement at Casiphia:* the site is unknown, but the interest here lies in the suggestion that the curious phrase 'the

place Casiphia' (repeated in the Hebrew where N.E.B. has
there) was a sanctuary. The word for 'place' came later to be
used in that sense, and the suggestion is likely. This would add
still more to the picture of the recruitment of Levites really
being a religious procession, part of the preparation for the
journey. Identification of Casiphia as a sanctuary would also
show that holy places other than Jerusalem were acceptable,
even to those who might be supposed to be the strongest
defenders of the claims of Jerusalem.

21. *I proclaimed a fast:* fasting as an appropriate preparation
for a religious task was characteristic of Judaism in the later
Old Testament period; there are several such references in the
books of Maccabees, and once again a parallel with Nehemiah
(Neh. 1: 4).

26–7. As in previous lists of sacred vessels, it is hard to take
the quantities literally: the total would run into millions of
pounds on modern reckoning. They seem to be rather a
picturesque way of emphasizing the importance of what was
transacted. The mention of only *two vessels of a fine red coppe.*
is a curious contrast. (The 'orichalc' of the N.E.B. footnote is
a yellow copper alloy.)

35. *seventy-two lambs:* the Hebrew text has 'seventy-seven'
(see N.E.B. footnote), but the change has been made because
of the Chronicler's fondness, particularly marked in this section, for the number twelve and its multiples, as expressive of
the wholeness of Israel. 'All Israel' has now *come home from
captivity*.

36. *They also delivered the king's commission:* this require-
ment, which may have been of considerable importance if
Ezra's original task was of a political nature, is not further
developed. It is possible, though it cannot be proved, that
Ezra had an official role in connection with the province of
Beyond-Euphrates (see the comment on 4: 9–10). ✳

THE PROBLEM OF MIXED MARRIAGES

9 When all this had been done, some of the leaders approached me and said, 'The people of Israel, including priests and Levites, have not kept themselves apart from the foreign population and from the abominable practices of the Canaanites, the Hittites, the Perizzites, the Jebusites, the Ammonites, the Moabites, the Egyptians,
2 and the Amorites. They have taken women of these nations as wives for themselves and their sons, so that the holy race has become mixed with the foreign population; and the leaders and magistrates have been the chief offen-
3 ders.' When I heard this news, I rent my robe and mantle, and tore my hair and my beard, and I sat dumbfounded;
4 and all who went in fear of the words of the God of Israel rallied to me because of the offence of these exiles. I sat there dumbfounded till the evening sacrifice.

5   Then, at the evening sacrifice, I rose from my humiliation and, in my rent robe and mantle, I knelt down and
6 spread out my hands to the LORD my God and said, 'O my God, I am humiliated, I am ashamed to lift my face to thee, my God; for we are sunk in our iniquities, and
7 our guilt is so great that it reaches high heaven. From the days of our fathers down to this present day our guilt has been great. For our iniquities we, our kings, and our priests have been subject to death, captivity, pillage, and shameful humiliation at the hands of foreign kings, and
8 such is our present plight. But now, for a brief moment, the LORD our God has been gracious to us, leaving us some survivors and giving us a foothold in his holy place. He has brought light to our eyes again and given us some

chance to renew our lives in our slavery. For slaves we 9
are; nevertheless, our God has not forsaken us in our
slavery, but has made the kings of Persia so well disposed
towards us as to give us the means of renewal, so that we
may repair the house of our God and rebuild its ruins, and
to give us a wall of defence in[a] Judah and Jerusalem. Now, 10
O our God, what are we to say after this? For we have
neglected the commands which thou gavest through thy 11
servants the prophets, when thou saidst, "The land which
you are entering and will possess is a polluted land,
polluted by the foreign population with their abominable
practices, which have made it unclean from end to end.
Therefore, do not give your daughters in marriage to 12
their sons, and do not marry your sons to their daughters,
and never seek their welfare or prosperity. Thus you will
be strong and enjoy the good things of the land, and pass
it on to your children as an everlasting possession." Now, 13
after all that we have suffered for our evil deeds and for
our great guilt – although thou, our God, hast punished
us less than our iniquities deserved and hast allowed us to
survive as now we do – shall we again disobey thy com- 14
mands and join in marriage with peoples who indulge in
such abominable practices? Would not thy anger against
us be unrelenting, until no remnant, no survivor was left?
O LORD God of Israel, thou art righteous; now as before, 15
we are only a remnant that has survived. Look upon us,
guilty as we are in thy sight; for because of our guilt none
of us can stand in thy presence.'

[a] *Or* thereby giving us a wall of defence for...

✣ Ezra's mission as described in the book of Ezra is concerned with the issue which is usually described as 'mixed marriages'. (Neh. 8 is dealt with in its present context, pp. 106–10.) To understand both the nature of the problem and the significance of Ezra's reaction to it, however, there are certain issues which need further clarification. First, we see that the Chronicler presents the return from exile as a new entry into the promised land, and reiterates the old warnings about contact with the existing inhabitants of the land. His concern is not, therefore, a new one, but the maintenance of a long-established tradition. Secondly, there have been clear examples earlier in his work of a welcome for those who were prepared to join themselves unreservedly to the covenant community (2 Chron. 30: 11; Ezra 6: 21). Thirdly, we shall need to keep in mind the question how far what is here described is a simple statement of what actually happened at a given moment in the community's history, and how far it is a stylized description of a ceremony which embodied those elements regarded as essential if the community were to retain its distinctiveness. A characteristic feature of the Old Testament is that the rigid rules laid down often appear to have been open to very varied interpretation in practice. More detailed points will emerge during the commentary on Ezra 9–10 and Neh. 13, but these general considerations need to be borne in mind throughout.

1. *When all this had been done:* though the first-person narrative continues, the connection with what has preceded is a very loose one. *the Canaanites...the Amorites:* lists of this kind are most familiar from the Pentateuch, and one such is used here in deliberate imitation of the earlier books. On frequent occasions in the Pentateuch a list of inhabitants of the promised land is given, with seven or occasionally eight nations being listed. The context is usually a warning to Israel to avoid all contact with these peoples (e.g. Deut. 7: 1). Two points are being made here. The first is that the return from exile is to be seen as a second exodus and entry into the promised land, and a list of this kind would provide just the

right kind of allusion to an audience familiar with the Pentateuch. Secondly, despite frequent warnings, Israel of old had
not kept free from entanglements with the native inhabitants,
and that danger has now arisen again. It is only possible to
keep clear of *the abominable practices* of these nations if the
people have *kept themselves apart* from them in all their life.
This is the basic rationale of what follows. Of the nations
listed, the first four are regularly found in the Pentateuchal
lists, and are included here to provide the appropriate association; they were no longer a menace in Ezra's day. Ammonites
and Moabites were traditional enemies of Israel, probably
mentioned here because of the specific condemnation of
association with them in Deut. 23: 3-6. The reference to
Egyptians and Amorites (another name for Canaanites) is less
easily explained, though Egypt was a traditional enemy and
Amorites may be an error for 'Edomites', another traditional
enemy, between whom and the Jews frequent wars were
waged.

2. *They have taken women of these nations as wives:* in these
books the offence always consists in taking foreign wives, not
of Israelite women marrying foreign husbands, though in
Deuteronomy both practices are condemned (Deut. 7: 3). We
see here the beginnings of the view that 'Jewishness' is trans-
mitted through the mother, which has remained a characteristic feature of Judaism. A New Testament example is
provided by Timothy (Acts 16: 1-3). *the holy race has become
mixed:* despite all the claims made for the universality of
Yahweh's power, there was still a very strong feeling that he
was the God of Israel. The failure to maintain racial purity
therefore inevitably involved religious malpractice.

3-4. Ezra's reaction should not be seen simply as a personal
reaction, though no doubt it was that; instead its primary
significance is as a ritual gesture, a solemn means of conveying
the seriousness of the situation.

5. Again there are set out the appropriate preparations for a
prayer of penitence: the rending of the robe, the kneeling for

prayer as expressive of contrition, and the spreading out of the hands.

6–15. Many of the elements in Ezra's prayer have a wider term of reference than the immediate crisis; God's kindness and the people's lack of response are set out, and then applied to the present situation. Thus, not all of the prayer seems to be addressed to God; part of it is an exhortation to the community to mend their ways. Another feature, characteristic of the prayers in the work of the Chronicler, is the use of allusions to earlier biblical passages, which would enable the reader to see similarities between the situation of his own community and that of the community addressed by earlier prophets. Thus, for example, verse 8 combines the two characteristic themes of the holy community and the holy place, and this is done by making reference on the one hand to God leaving some survivors – the word is the same as that translated 'remnant' in prophetic passages such as Isa. 10: 20–2 – and on the other by an allusion to Isa. 22: 23–5 contained in the word translated by N.E.B. here as *foothold* and there as 'peg'. The community of Ezra's day is thus identified, both for promise and warning, with those to whom the prophets had spoken in their day. (For a fuller consideration of the same principles, see 2 Chron. 20 in the commentary on 1 and 2 Chronicles in this series.)

6–7. Ezra associates himself with the guilt of the people, to a much greater extent than the Chronicler's own history had done, and stresses their continuing wickedness, which had led to punishment. There is no place here for the earlier period of favour under David.

9. *has made the kings of Persia so well disposed towards us:* a recurrent theme of the whole book, and a marked contrast to the attitude of earlier Old Testament writers to other foreign powers. *we may repair the house of our God:* again the unity of the whole restoration epoch is envisaged, Ezra's work being taken as one with the restoration of the temple. *a wall of defence:* the phrase is probably metaphorical, but in any case

it would be risky to attempt to correlate it in any way with
Nehemiah's rebuilding of the city walls, because a different
Hebrew word is used, and the reference here is to *Judah and
Jerusalem*.

10–11. *the commands which thou gavest through thy servants the
prophets:* what follows is not a direct quotation from any
prophetic passage, but contains allusions to several earlier Old
Testament passages, notably Deut. 7: 1–6. But all earlier
writings which were regarded as authoritative came to be
regarded as prophetic, and applicable to the situation in the
interpreter's own day.

13–14. These verses, though formally still addressed to
God, are clearly intended as an exhortation to the people, and
apply much more precisely than what has preceded to the
immediate subject of anxiety – the joining *in marriage with
peoples who indulge in such abominable practices.*

15. The prayer concludes with a direct appeal to God, and
the use once again of the theme of a *remnant*, again possibly
based on earlier prophetic collections. ✲

THE REFORM CARRIED OUT

While Ezra was praying and making confession, pros- **10**
trate in tears before the house of God, a very great crowd
of Israelites assembled round him, men, women, and
children, and they all wept bitterly. Then Shecaniah son 2
of Jehiel, one of the family of Elam, spoke up and said to
Ezra, 'We have committed an offence against our God in
marrying foreign wives, daughters of the foreign population. But in spite of this, there is still hope for Israel. Now, 3
therefore, let us pledge ourselves to our God to dismiss all
these women and their brood, according to your advice,
my lord, and the advice of those who go in fear of the
command of our God; and let us act as the law prescribes.

4 Up now, the task is yours, and we will support you. Take courage and act.'

5 Ezra stood up and made the chiefs of the priests, the Levites, and all the Israelites swear to do as had been said;
6 and they took the oath. Then Ezra left his place in front of the house of God and went to the room of Jehohanan grandson*a* of Eliashib and lodged*b* there; he neither ate bread nor drank water, for he was mourning for the
7 offence committed by the exiles who had returned. Next, there was issued throughout Judah and Jerusalem a proclamation that all the exiles should assemble in Jerusalem,
8 and that if anyone did not arrive within three days, it should be within the discretion of the chief officers and the elders to confiscate*c* all his property and to exclude
9 him from the community of the exiles. So all the men of Judah and Benjamin assembled in Jerusalem within the three days; and on the twentieth day of the ninth month the people all sat in the forecourt of the house of God, trembling with apprehension and shivering in the heavy
10 rain. Ezra the priest stood up and said, 'You have committed an offence in marrying foreign wives and have
11 added to Israel's guilt. Make your confession now to the LORD the God of your fathers and do his will, and separate yourselves from the foreign population and from your
12 foreign wives.' Then all the assembled people shouted in
13 reply, 'Yes; we must do what you say. But there is a great crowd of us here, and it is the rainy season; we cannot go on standing out here in the open. Besides, this business will not be finished in one day or even two,

[a] *Lit.* son.   [b] *Prob. rdg., cp. 1 Esdras 9: 2; Heb.* went.
[c] *Lit.* to devote.

because we have committed so grave an offence in this matter. Let our leading men act for the whole assembly, 14 and let all in our cities who have married foreign women present themselves at appointed times, each man with the elders and judges of his own city, until God's anger against us on this account[a] is averted.' Only Jonathan son of 15 Asahel and Jahzeiah son of Tikvah, supported by Meshullam and Shabbethai the Levite, opposed this.

So the exiles acted as agreed, and Ezra the priest 16 selected[b] certain men, heads of households representing their families, all of them designated by name. They began their formal inquiry into the matter on the first day of the tenth month, and by the first day of the first month 17 they had finished their inquiry into all the marriages with foreign women.

Among the members of priestly families who had mar- 18 ried foreign women were found Maaseiah, Eliezer, Jarib, and Gedaliah of the family of Jeshua son of Jozadak and his brothers. They pledged themselves to dismiss their 19 wives, and they brought a ram from the flock as a guilt-offering for their sins. Of the family of Immer: Hanani 20 and Zebadiah. Of the family of Harim: Maaseiah, Elijah, 21 Shemaiah, Jehiel and Uzziah. Of the family of Pashhur: 22 Elioenai, Maaseiah, Ishmael, Nethaneel, Jozabad and Elasah.

Of the Levites: Jozabad, Shimei, Kelaiah (that is Kelita), 23 Pethahiah, Judah and Eliezer. Of the singers: Eliashib. Of 24 the door-keepers: Shallum, Telem and Uri.

And of Israel: of the family of Parosh: Ramiah, Izziah, 25

[a] on this account: *so Pesh.; Heb.* as far as this.
[b] and Ezra the priest selected: *prob. rdg., cp. 1 Esdras 9: 16; Heb. obscure.*

26 Malchiah, Mijamin, Eleazar, Malchiah and Benaiah. Of the family of Elam: Mattaniah, Zechariah, Jehiel, Abdi,
27 Jeremoth and Elijah. Of the family of Zattu: Elioenai,
28 Eliashib, Mattaniah, Jeremoth, Zabad and Aziza. Of the family of Bebai: Jehohanan, Hananiah, Zabbai and Athlai.
29 Of the family of Bani: Meshullam, Malluch, Adaiah,
30 Jashub, Sheal and Jeremoth. Of the family of Pahath-moab: Adna, Kelal, Benaiah, Maaseiah, Mattaniah,
31 Bezalel, Binnui and Manasseh. Of*a* the family of Harim:
32 Eliezer, Isshijah, Malchiah, Shemaiah, Simeon, Benjamin,
33 Malluch and Shemariah. Of the family of Hashum: Mattenai, Mattattah, Zabad, Eliphelet, Jeremai, Manasseh
34 and Shimei. Of the family of Bani: Maadai, Amram and
35, 36 Uel, Benaiah, Bedeiah and Keluhi, Vaniah, Meremoth,
37, 38 Eliashib, Mattaniah, Mattenai and Jaasau. Of the family
39 of*b* Binnui: Shimei, Shelemiah, Nathan and Adaiah,
40, 41 Maknadebai, Shashai and Sharai, Azareel, Shelemiah and
42, 43 Shemariah, Shallum, Amariah and Joseph. Of the family of Nebo: Jeiel, Mattithiah, Zabad, Zebina, Jaddai, Joel and
44 Benaiah. All these had married foreign women, and they dismissed them, together with their children.*c*

* The material relating to the putting away of foreign wives reverts to the third person, as in ch. 7. It may be possible to regard this simply as a stylistic device, but it is also possible that another source has here been incorporated into the narrative. The parallels with Nehemiah, already noted several times, are carried a stage further, for Ezra's action here is

[a] *So many MSS.; others om.*
[b] *Of the family of: prob. rdg., cp. 1 Esdras 9: 34; Heb. and Bani and.*
[c] *and they...children: prob. rdg., cp. 1 Esdras 9: 36; Heb. and some of them were women; and they had borne sons.*

closely parallel to that carried out by Nehemiah in Neh. 13:
23–30. Rather than speculate about possible historical circumstances which necessitated the same action being performed
twice, it is better to think of the same action being described in
varying forms in different traditions.

1–4. Zeal for establishing the true community is not confined to Ezra and the priestly ranks alone; here Shecaniah,
apparently a layman, acknowledges guilt on behalf of the
community and its willingness to take appropriate action. In
verse 3 the N.E.B. has, by a slight change, made *my lord* refer
to Ezra rather than to God, as in the Hebrew text.

5. *the priests, the Levites, and all the Israelites:* this is the
threefold manner of describing the total community regularly
found in Ezra.

6. *Jehohanan grandson of Eliashib:* this reference has played
an important, perhaps an exaggerated, part, in attempts to
resolve the chronological problem concerning Ezra and
Nehemiah. It rests on the identification of the Jehohanan mentioned here with the 'Jonathan' or 'Johanan' of Neh. 12: 11,
22. If Nehemiah's mission is dated 445 B.C., then it would
seem likely that Ezra's commission should be placed under
Artaxerxes II, in 398 B.C. In fact, this cannot so readily be
assumed. In addition to the fact that Nehemiah's date is less
certain than is commonly maintained, it is to be noted that the
identification here envisaged is not firmly established. The
name in Nehemiah is not certain, and the forms 'Jonathan'
and 'Johanan' differ significantly in Hebrew. Again, the
N.E.B. translation *grandson* is based on a comparison with
Neh. 12, the Hebrew text here reading 'son' as is indicated by
N.E.B. footnote, and is no more than a conjecture, since both
Johanan and Eliashib were common names. One of the
papyri from Elephantine which have already been referred to
(see p. 7) refers to 'the High Priest Johanan' at about 410 B.C.,
but we have no means of knowing whether the same figure is
referred to here. In short, we may conclude that this verse
fits in well with the theory that puts Ezra some fifty years

after Nehemiah but is far from establishing it. *he neither ate bread nor drank water, for he was mourning:* it is not clear why this ascetic preparation should be repeated. Perhaps the tradition here is a variant form of that already set out in ch. 9. *committed by the exiles:* throughout this section it is noteworthy that it is the returned exiles who are the object of concern. They are the true community; they should the more readily have recognized the folly of their action.

7–8. It is envisaged that those concerned were a recognizable group, able to assemble in this way.

9. *the men of Judah and Benjamin:* the text here reverts to this usage, as in ch. 1, as against the 'all Israel' usage of most of the book. *shivering in the heavy rain:* Jerusalem in the winter (*the ninth month*) can be extremely cold, and snow is not uncommon.

10–14. Ezra's appeal meets a ready response, and the narrative here is markedly less stylized than in much of the Chronicler's material. Whereas many statements of apparent fact appear to have a primarily theological motivation, it is unlikely that this is so of the climatic note repeated here.

15. Just as Nehemiah's campaign against mixed marriages led to a clash with a priestly family (Neh. 13: 28), so some opposition to Ezra is recorded, with a Levite involved. As so often is the case, it is unlikely that any of the names recorded in lists of this kind can confidently be identified with those mentioned elsewhere. It has sometimes been argued that the opposition was not to Ezra's measures as such, but to the means of carrying them out: the Hebrew text is somewhat ambiguous at this point.

16–17. The procedure for establishing more precisely who were at fault is now set out. Apparently a lay commission is established; the Hebrew text is obscure, as the N.E.B. footnote indicates, and the reference in it to Ezra may be secondary. In three months a list of offenders is drawn up.

18–44. The book ends on what is for us a curious note of anti-climax with a list of names of those who had married

64

foreign wives. It can scarcely be said of such a list, as it can of those at the beginning of 1 Chronicles, that lists of names could be interpreted as showing the course of the divine favour, for this list consists of those who had fallen away. It is probably relevant to bear in mind that there is still one more aspect of Ezra's work to be related, namely the reading of the book of the law in Neh. 8. It is possible that that ceremony is put last in the description of Ezra's achievement, so as to provide the appropriate conclusion.

Among the names in these verses there are several that are probably to be identified with those that have been mentioned elsewhere, but it seems likely that we have access here to another source underlying the Chronicler's work. The list is divided into what has by now come to be the customary grouping of priests, Levites and 'Israel', that is, what we should call the laity.

18–22. The priestly families listed here are related to the list of priestly families in 2: 36–9.

19. This ceremony of cleansing is only described for the priests. It is not clear whether we are to assume that a similar ceremony was performed by all who had offended, or whether the sin of the priests was regarded as more heinous and stricter observance was therefore necessary. Stricter requirements for priests may be found in other contexts, for example, in regard to contact with the dead (cp. Lev. 21: 1–4, and the rules in the remainder of that chapter).

23–4. Unlike the priestly names, those of the *Levites*, *singers* and *door-keepers* are not found elsewhere.

25–43. The majority of these family names can be traced in the list in ch. 2, but there are a number of uncertainties, particularly at the end of the list, where such names as *Maknadebai* (verse 40) and *Nebo* (the name of a Babylonian god? – verse 43) are not Hebrew words. Confusion in the transmission of lists of names is always a hazard.

44. As the N.E.B. footnote inducates, the original of this verse differs markedly from the version adopted; little sense

can be made of the original and the suggestion of N.E.B. is as
likely as any. To us, the fact that children were involved
heightens the objectionable nature of the proceedings, but we
have no knowledge of the subsequent fate of those concerned,
which it was not part of the Chronicler's purpose to relate. ✳

✳   ✳   ✳   ✳   ✳   ✳   ✳   ✳   ✳   ✳   ✳   ✳   ✳

THE BOOK OF

NEHEMIAH

✳   ✳   ✳   ✳   ✳   ✳   ✳   ✳   ✳   ✳   ✳   ✳   ✳

THE ARRANGEMENT OF THE MATERIAL

If the arrangement of material in the book of Ezra at times seems puzzling, that in Nehemiah presents even greater difficulties. It begins clearly enough (1: 1–7: 5), with what has usually been called the 'memoir of Nehemiah', but we have seen already (above, p. 4) that it may more appropriately be regarded as a memorial to Nehemiah. This leads into an extended list (7: 6–73), which is virtually identical with the list of returning exiles in Ezra 2. There follows a sentence describing an assembly of the people just as in Ezra 3: 1, but this time the sequel is entirely different – a description of Ezra's reading of the book of the law. Nehemiah himself is mentioned in this chapter (8: 9), but it is likely that this is only a secondary addition to link the two men together (see the commentary). Chs. 9 and 10 are extremely difficult to assign to their original setting with any confidence. Ch. 9 is substantially a long prayer of repentance, ch. 10 a ceremony of covenant-renewal. There has long been debate among scholars concerning the relation of these chapters to one another and to the remainder of the material concerned with Ezra and Nehemiah. All that can be said here is that these chapters appear to have reached their present position as rounding off the Ezra tradition, but that originally they may well have been separate pieces of tradition available to the Chronicler but not connected with either Ezra or Nehemiah.

The greater part of chs. 11 and 12 is given over to further lists of names but the last verses (12: 27–43) bring us back to the first-person source, possibly the same as that found in chs. 1-6, and this is also found in ch. 13, which describes a second mission of Nehemiah some years later than his first.

Since some of the first-person material is also interspersed with sections that appear to come from a different source (e.g. ch. 3, with its description of the repairing of the walls), it seems most likely that the Chronicler has drawn together here, as in Ezra, a variety of different sources so as to present an overall picture of the restoration of the community in Jerusalem. In these circumstances, we should be cautious in attempting to reconstruct the precise course of historical events, the more so because, as has been seen, we cannot be certain of the date of either Ezra or Nehemiah.

✻ ✻ ✻ ✻ ✻ ✻ ✻ ✻ ✻ ✻ ✻ ✻ ✻

Nehemiah's commission

THE DISTRESS OF GOD'S PEOPLE AND CITY

1 THE NARRATIVE OF NEHEMIAH son of Hacaliah. In the month Kislev in the twentieth year, when I was
2 in Susa the capital city, it happened that one of my brothers, Hanani, arrived with some others from Judah; and I asked them about Jerusalem and about the Jews, the families still remaining of those who survived the cap-
3 tivity. They told me that those still remaining in the province who had survived the captivity were facing great trouble and reproach; the wall of Jerusalem was broken down and the gates had been destroyed by fire.
4 When I heard this news, I sat down and wept; I mourned for some days, fasting and praying to the God of heaven.
5 This was my prayer: 'O LORD God of heaven, O great and terrible God who faithfully keepest covenant with

those who love thee and observe thy commandments, let 6
thy ear be attentive and thine eyes open, to hear my
humble prayer which I make to thee day and night on
behalf of thy servants the sons of Israel. I confess the sins
which we Israelites have all committed against thee, and
of which I and my father's house are also guilty. We have 7
wronged thee and have not observed the commandments,
statutes, and rules which thou didst enjoin upon thy servant Moses. Remember what thou didst impress upon 8
him in these words: "If you are unfaithful, I will disperse
you among the nations; but if you return to me and 9
observe my commandments and fulfil them, I will gather
your children who have been scattered to the ends of the
earth and will bring them home to the place which I have
chosen as a dwelling for my Name." They are thy ser- 10
vants and thy people, whom thou hast redeemed with thy
great might and thy strong hand. O Lord, let thy ear be 11a
attentive to my humble prayer, and to the prayer of thy
servants who delight to revere thy name. Grant me good
success this day, and put it into this man's heart to show
me kindness.'

* Though the Hebrew Bible prints Ezra and Nehemiah as
one continuous work, the introduction to Nehemiah shows
that it is originally part of a separate tradition. There is no
account taken here of the work of restoration which has been
described in Ezra; instead, we are back in a situation where
'the wall of Jerusalem was broken down and the gates had
been destroyed by fire' (verse 3). This introductory chapter as
a whole bears marked similarities to a prophet's call – it is
described as 'the words of Nehemiah' (verse 1: the N.E.B.
translation, 'narrative of Nehemiah', though possible in itself,

destroys this link with similar introductions such as Jer. 1: 1);
it contains the characteristic response on the part of the one
called that the burden is too great (verse 4; cp. Jer. 1: 6),
together with a prayer of repentance and a self-identification
of the one called with the whole community. The prophetic
link may be, not so much with Nehemiah as an individual, as
with the collection of material relating to him. Probably when
this reached its final form, the prophetic collections were also
becoming important, and this was consciously shaped in a
similar way.

1. *Nehemiah son of Hacaliah:* nothing is known of him or
his family save what we are told here, and he is not given the
extended genealogy which was thought appropriate for the
priest Ezra.

In the month Kislev: this is the same 'ninth month' as is
mentioned in Ezra 10: 9. From about the sixth century B.C.
Israel came to accept the Babylonian practice of beginning the
year in the spring instead of the autumn, and also took over
the Babylonian names for the months. Kislev came in
November–December. *in the twentieth year:* presumably that
of King Artaxerxes (cp. 2: 1). This introduces further chronological difficulty, since Kislev is later in the year than 'Nisan'
(March–April) mentioned in 2: 1. *Susa the capital city:* already
referred to in Ezra 4: 9 as one of the chief Persian cities, it was
the winter capital, situated near the head of the Persian Gulf.

2. *Hanani:* most probably the same as the brother of
Nehemiah referred to in 7: 2. *the Jews:* elsewhere the N.E.B
has translated the same Hebrew word by 'Judaeans' (e.g.
2 Kings 16: 6); but the rendering *Jews*, denoting a religious
community rather than the inhabitants of a particular area, is
probably correct here. *the families still remaining of those who
survived the captivity:* the phrase is ambiguous, both in Hebrew
and English. It could mean those who had returned from
exile, but it seems more likely here – as against Ezra – to
refer to those who had not been in Babylon. There is little
in the material relating to Nehemiah which is concerned

with the issues of exile and return which are so prominent in
Ezra.

3. *the wall of Jerusalem was broken down and the gates had been
destroyed by fire:* two quite different types of interpretation are
possible here. Those who regard this material as a genuine
'memoir' of Nehemiah will see in this an allusion to some
recent disaster which had befallen Jerusalem – perhaps that
referred to in Ezra 4: 8–23, which is dated in the time of
Artaxerxes. Those who take this to be a later idealization of
Nehemiah's work will be more likely to see the beginnings
of that foreshortening of the time perspective clearly visible in
2 Macc. 1: 18, where Nehemiah is presented as belonging to
the first generation of those who restored the city. In that case,
the allusion here would be to the destruction of Jerusalem by
the Babylonians in 587/6. Unfortunately, there is no un-
ambiguous witness from archaeology which might help
towards a decisive answer to this uncertainty.

5–11. The prayer of Nehemiah is full of phrases regularly
found in such expressions of penitence in the Old Testament.
In particular, many of the phrases found here have very close
parallels in the book of Deuteronomy. The prayer is for the
most part unrelated to any specific context; only in the last
phrase (*this man*, verse 11, which in the Hebrew is the very last
phrase) is reference made to the immediate object of the
prayer. ✷

THE KING COMMISSIONS NEHEMIAH

Now I was the king's cupbearer, and one day, in the 11*b*.
month Nisan, in the twentieth year of King Artaxerxes,
when his wine was ready, I took it up and handed it to the
king, and as I stood before him I was feeling very unhappy. He said to me, 'Why do you look so unhappy? 2
You are not ill; it can be nothing but unhappiness.' I was
much afraid and answered, 'The king will live for ever. 3

But how can I help looking unhappy when the city where my forefathers are buried lies waste and its gates are 4 burnt?' 'What are you asking of me?' said the king. I 5 prayed to the God of heaven, and then I answered, 'If it please your majesty, and if I enjoy your favour, I beg you to send me to Judah, to the city where my forefathers are 6 buried, so that I may rebuild it.' The king, with the queen consort sitting beside him, asked me, 'How long will the journey last, and when will you return?' Then the king approved the request and let me go, and I told him how 7 long I should be. Then I said to the king, 'If it please your majesty, let letters be given me for the governors in the province of Beyond-Euphrates with orders to grant me 8 all the help I need for my journey to Judah. Let me have also a letter for Asaph, the keeper of your royal forests, instructing him to supply me with timber to make beams for the gates of the citadel, which adjoins the palace, and for the city wall, and for the palace which I shall occupy.' The king granted my requests, for the gracious hand of 9 my God was upon me. I came in due course to the governors in the province of Beyond-Euphrates and presented to them the king's letters; the king had given me 10 an escort of army officers with cavalry. But when Sanballat the Horonite and the slave Tobiah, an Ammonite, heard this, they were much vexed that someone should have come to promote the interests of the Israelites.

* The N.E.B. rightly prints the last phrase of ch. 1 with the narrative that follows, which tells of the success of Nehemiah's approach to the king. This section sets the scene for what is to follow: the divine favour, shown through the support of the

Persian king and imperial authorities, and the opposition personified in Sanballat and Tobiah. The remainder of the material relating to Nehemiah will show his work is carried out, with the divine favour, and despite all human opposition.

11*b*. *I was the king's cupbearer:* such a position, which involved tasting any drink to avoid attempts to poison the king, was most frequently held by a eunuch. Nehemiah may have been such, but there is no specific indication of it, unless we are to think that the writing of a 'memorial' was designed to keep his name alive, since he would have no descendant.

2: 1. *in the twentieth year of King Artaxerxes:* if the king referred to is Artaxerxes I (465–424 B.C.), the date will have been 445; if Artaxerxes II (404–358 B.C.), it was 384. The first is more likely, but certainty is impossible.

1–4. The language in these verses is extremely stylized and it is unwise to construct from it theories as to Nehemiah's personal psychology. The point is recognized by the king as leading to a request.

6. *the queen consort sitting beside him:* no further explanation is given of this detail, which might be a further pointer to the supposition that Nehemiah was a eunuch. *the king approved the request:* that we are here in the realm of the skilful narrator rather than of prosaic statement of facts is further illustrated by the point that the details of Nehemiah's mission are not given here; the remainder of the narrative is used to show just what he was to achieve.

7–8. The requests for co-operation from the imperial officials are reminiscent of the arrangements made for Ezra's journey (Ezra 7: 21–4). It is difficult to know how far this correspondence is due to the fact that both men were in fact engaged on very similar tasks, and how far an editorial hand has stressed the correspondence.

10. *Sanballat the Horonite:* he is presented throughout as the leader of the opposition to Nehemiah. His rank is not here stated, but in a papyrus from Elephantine in Egypt, dating from about 410 B.C., a reference is made to 'the sons of Sanballat

the governor of Samaria', and it is likely that this was his office. It used to be supposed that this reference meant that Nehemiah could confidently be dated under Artaxerxes I, since it would fit well chronologically for an active governor in 445 to have delegated responsibility to his sons by 410; but the position has been confused by the discovery of other papyri, at Wadi Daliyeh near the Jordan, that refer to another Sanballat who must have been active in the early fourth century; and it is possible that this was Nehemiah's enemy. *Sanballat* is a Babylonian name (Sin-uballit, or 'Sin [the moon god] gives life'), but both the Sanballats known from papyrus discoveries had sons with Yahwistic names, and it is noteworthy that the condemnation of Sanballat here never refers to religious practice. There are various places of which 'horon' was part of the name, so we cannot be sure of the exact place designated by *Horonite. the slave Tobiah, an Ammonite:* in its present form, especially as translated by the N.E.B., this description of Nehemiah's second adversary is clearly meant to be derogatory. He is both a slave and also a member of a hostile foreign nation, an Ammonite. But it is also possible that the word translated *slave* could be rendered 'servant' and that the real meaning is that Tobiah was an imperial official, and that *Ammonite* may refer not to his racial origins but to his holding some official position in the old Ammonite territory east of the Jordan. His name, *Tobiah,* 'the LORD is my good', is a good Yahwistic name (cp. Ezra 2: 60), and it is noteworthy that in the third and second centuries B.C., under the Ptolemies and Seleucids, there was a prominent family of Jews known as the Tobiads. It is tempting but unprovable to see their ancestor in this Tobiah. (For an outline of the importance of the Tobiad family at this later date, see the commentary on 1 and 2 Maccabees in this series, p. 4.) *they were much vexed:* understandably enough. From their point of view it would appear that Nehemiah's commission would diminish their own position and that political tension, which to them might seem unnecessary, was now inevitable. They no doubt shared the view of the complainants in Ezra 4: 12–16, that Jerusalem's past history proved how troublesome a city it had been, and that any attempt at rebuilding the walls would only exacerbate old rivalries. *

The walls of Jerusalem rebuilt

* The N.E.B. uses this sub-heading to describe the whole of the remainder of Neh. 2–7, though in fact various other themes are found in these chapters. *

NEHEMIAH'S TOUR OF INSPECTION

W HEN I ARRIVED in Jerusalem, I waited three days. 11 Then I set out by night, taking a few men with me; 12 but I told no one what my God was prompting me to do for Jerusalem. I had no beast with me except the one on which I myself rode. I went out by night through the 13 Valley Gate towards the Dragon Spring and the Dung Gate, and I inspected the places where the walls of Jerusalem had been broken down and her gates burnt. Then I 14 passed on to the Fountain Gate and the King's Pool; but there was no room for me to ride through. I went up the 15 valley in the night and inspected the city wall; then I re-entered the city by the Valley Gate. So I arrived back without the magistrates knowing where I had been or 16 what I was doing. I had not yet told the Jews, the priests, the nobles, the magistrates, or any of those who would be responsible for the work.

Then I said to them, 'You see our wretched plight. 17 Jerusalem lies in ruins, its gates destroyed by fire. Come,

let us rebuild the wall of Jerusalem and be rid of the
18 reproach.' I told them how the gracious hand of my God
had been upon me and also what the king had said to me.
They replied, 'Let us start the rebuilding.' So they set
about the work vigorously and to good purpose.

19   But when Sanballat the Horonite, Tobiah the Ammonite slave, and Geshem the Arab heard of it, they jeered at
us, asking contemptuously, 'What is this you are doing?
20 Is this a rebellion against the king?' But I answered them,
'The God of heaven will give us success. We, his servants,
are making a start with the rebuilding. You have no
stake, or claim, or traditional right in Jerusalem.'

✳ These opening verses describe Nehemiah's inspection of
the city, and make it clear that opposition is inevitable. Unfortunately our knowledge of the topography of Jerusalem is
not sufficient for us to be able to describe the exact route taken
by Nehemiah. The identity of the site of Jerusalem has never
been lost sight of, as has happened with so many other ancient
cities where modern archaeologists have been at work; but
the long period of occupation makes it impossible to reconstruct the state of the city with confidence at any one
particular period. The number of identifications suggested on
the plan (see p. 77) has therefore been limited.

11. *I waited three days:* one of the many small details in
which Ezra's and Nehemiah's work are described in exactly
similar terms (cp. Ezra 8: 15).

13. *the Valley Gate:* referred to in 2 Chron. 26: 9, and twice
more in Nehemiah, but impossible to identify with certainty.
It is highly probable that Nehemiah's expedition took place
at the southern end of the city, but we cannot be more precise.

16. *without the magistrates knowing:* the reference is probably
not to Sanballat and Tobiah, but either to Persian officials in
Jerusalem or to the other Jewish leaders.

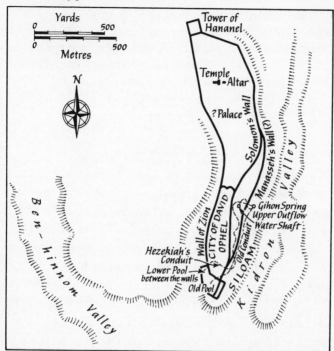

Map of Jerusalem. The map gives an approximate outline of Jerusalem in the monarchical period. Already before the exile there had been westward extensions of the city, but the size of the area involved is not known. The places mentioned in Neh. 2 and 3 will have included part of this western extension.

17–18. As with Ezra's appeal in the matter of mixed marriages, Nehemiah's appeal here meets with instant response.

19. *Geshem the Arab:* the third of Nehemiah's opponents is introduced here for the first time. Again it seems most probable that he was an official in charge of an area of the Persian Empire, possibly some form of Arab confederacy to the south and east of Judah.

Is this a rebellion against the king?: again the question is in itself a reasonable one, for a major rebuilding of Jerusalem could obviously be interpreted as treasonable, but it is treated by Nehemiah as an opportunity for affirming the rights of the Jews to their own holy city, and that these rulers of other neighbouring lands had 'no stake, or claim, or traditional right in Jerusalem' (verse 20). ✳

DETAILS OF THE REPAIR

3 Eliashib the high priest and his fellow-priests started work and rebuilt the Sheep Gate. They laid its beams[a] and set its doors in place; they carried the work as far as the Tower of the Hundred, as far as the Tower of Hananel,
2 and consecrated it. Next to Eliashib the men of Jericho worked; and next to them Zaccur son of Imri.

3 The Fish Gate was built by the sons of Hassenaah; they laid its tie-beams and set its doors in place with their bolts
4 and bars. Next to them Meremoth son of Uriah, son of Hakkoz, repaired his section; next to them Meshullam son of Berechiah, son of Meshezabel; next to them Zadok
5 son of Baana did the repairs; and next again the men of Tekoa did the repairs, but their nobles would not demean themselves to serve their governor.

6 The Jeshanah Gate[b] was repaired by Joiada son of Paseah and Meshullam son of Besodeiah; they laid its tie-beams and set its doors in place with their bolts and bars.
7 Next to them Melatiah the Gibeonite and Jadon the Meronothite, the men of Gibeon and Mizpah, did the repairs as far as the seat of the governor of the province of
8 Beyond-Euphrates. Next to them Uzziel son of Harhaiah,

[a] laid its beams: *prob. rdg.; Heb.* consecrated it.
[b] The Jeshanah Gate: *or* The gate of the Old City.

a goldsmith,[a] did the repairs, and next Hananiah, a perfumer; they reconstructed Jerusalem as far as the Broad
Wall. Next to them Rephaiah son of Hur, ruler of half 9
the district of Jerusalem, did the repairs. Next to them 10
Jedaiah son of Harumaph did the repairs opposite his own
house; and next Hattush son of Hashabniah. Malchiah 11
son of Harim and Hasshub son of Pahath-moab repaired
a second section including the Tower of the Ovens.[b] Next 12
to them Shallum son of Hallohesh, ruler of half the district
of Jerusalem, did the repairs with the help of his daughters.

The Valley Gate was repaired by Hanun and the in- 13
habitants of Zanoah; they rebuilt it and set its doors in
place with their bolts and bars, and they repaired a thousand cubits of the wall as far as the Dung Gate. The Dung 14
Gate itself was repaired by Malchiah son of Rechab, ruler
of the district of Beth-hakkerem; he rebuilt[c] it and set its
doors in place with their bolts and bars. The Fountain 15
Gate was repaired by Shallun[d] son of Col-hozeh, ruler of
the district of Mizpah; he rebuilt[c] it and roofed it and set
its doors in place with their bolts and bars; and he built
the wall of the Pool of Shelah next to the king's garden
and onwards as far as the steps leading down from the
City of David.

After him Nehemiah son of Azbuk, ruler of half the 16
district of Beth-zur, did the repairs as far as a point opposite the burial-place of David, as far as the artificial pool
and the House of the Heroes.[e] After him the Levites did 17
the repairs: Rehum son of Bani and next to him Hasha-

[a] a goldsmith: *so Pesh.; Heb.* goldsmiths.
[b] *Or* Furnaces.   [c] *Prob. rdg.; Heb.* he will rebuild.
[d] *Or, with some MSS.,* Shallum.   [e] *Or* and the barracks.

biah, ruler of half the district of Keilah, did the repairs for
18 his district. After him their kinsmen did the repairs:
Binnui[a] son of Henadad, ruler of half the district of
19 Keilah; next to him Ezer son of Jeshua, ruler of Mizpah,
repaired a second section opposite the point at which the
20 ascent meets the escarpment; after him Baruch son of
Zabbai[b] repaired a second section, from the escarpment
21 to the door of the house of Eliashib the high priest. After
him Meremoth son of Uriah, son of Hakkoz, repaired a
second section, from the door of the house of Eliashib to
the end of the house of Eliashib.

22 After him the priests of the neighbourhood of Jerusa-
23 lem did the repairs. Next Benjamin and Hasshub did the
repairs opposite their own house; and next Azariah son
of Maaseiah, son of Ananiah, did the repairs beside his
24 house. After him Binnui son of Henadad repaired a second
section, from the house of Azariah as far as the escarpment
25 and the corner. Palal son of Uzai worked opposite the
escarpment and the upper tower which projects from the
26 king's house and belongs to the court of the guard. After
him Pedaiah son of Parosh[c] worked as far as a point on
the east opposite the Water Gate and the projecting tower.
27 Next the men of Tekoa repaired a second section, from a
point opposite the great projecting tower as far as the
wall of Ophel.

28 Above the Horse Gate the priests did the repairs oppo-
29 site their own houses. After them Zadok son of Immer did
the repairs opposite his own house; after him Shemaiah

[a] *So some MSS.; others* Bavvai.
[b] *So some MSS.; others add* inflamed.
[c] *Prob. rdg.; Heb. adds* and the temple-servitors lodged on Ophel
(*cp. 11: 21*).

son of Shecaniah, the keeper of the East Gate, did the
repairs. After him Hananiah son of Shelemiah and Hanun, 30
sixth son of Zalaph, repaired a second section. After him
Meshullam son of Berechiah did the repairs opposite his
room. After him Malchiah, a goldsmith, did the repairs 31
as far as the house of the temple-servitors[a] and the merchants, opposite the Mustering Gate, as far as the roof-
chamber at the corner. Between the roof-chamber at the 32
corner and the Sheep Gate the goldsmiths and merchants
did the repairs.

* The details concerning those who rebuilt the walls, which
make up this chapter, are appropriately added here, but they
are unlikely to have formed any part of the original block of
Nehemiah material. Nehemiah himself is not named; the list
starts extremely abruptly, and there are no references to any
of the people or incidents from the Nehemiah tradition. Some
form of archival record of this enterprise may have been available, or more likely, a series of partial records, since there are
a number of gaps and inconsistencies within the list as it now
stands. For those interested in topography this is one of the
most tantalizing chapters in the Bible, for if we could interpret
the information given in it with confidence, we should be able
to add very greatly to our knowledge of Jerusalem at this
period. But though it seems likely that a complete circum-
ference of the city walls is described, since 'the Sheep Gate' is
both the starting and finishing point (verses 1 and 32), and
though a few places can be identified with some confidence,
far too much remains uncertain for any total picture to be
built up.

1. *Eliashib the high priest:* if this Eliashib is the same as the
one referred to in 12: 10 (and the genealogy there is accurate)

[a] *Heb.* Nethinim.

then we should be able to date Nehemiah with fair certainty under Artaxerxes I, since Eliashib is said to be the grandson of Jeshua, who was high priest about 520 B.C. But the name is a common one and the identification uncertain.

They laid its beams: the N.E.B. has made a slight emendation of the Hebrew to obtain this reading. But the Hebrew 'they consecrated it' (see the N.E.B. footnote) is also possible; it might well be thought appropriate that the whole proceedings should begin with a religious ceremony. *Tower of the Hundred* and *Tower of Hananel* appear to be alternative names for the same tower. The N.E.B. translation here is ambiguous.

2. *the men of Jericho:* whereas the list in ch. 7 (found also in Ezra 2) appears to set out personal names and place-names separately, in this list they are intermingled.

3. *The Fish Gate:* mentioned also in 2 Chron. 33: 14, and from the context there probably to be placed in the northern part of the city. It is almost certain that the gates are described in a counter-clockwise direction.

4. *repaired:* this word is used many times in this chapter, but it is very general in meaning, and we cannot be certain how extensive were the works involved. The idea expressed by the verb in question is simply 'to make firm or strong'.

5. *their nobles would not demean themselves to serve their governor:* this is the only section in the chapter suggestive of a lack of whole-hearted co-operation, and this is doubly curious because *the men of Tekoa* (the home of the prophet Amos, but otherwise not mentioned in Ezra–Nehemiah) repaired a second section (verse 27). *their governor* could equally be understood as their lord, i.e. God, as in the Revised Standard Version.

6. *The Jeshanah Gate:* other English versions have 'the old gate'; it is referred to again in 12: 39, but the site is unknown.

7. *as far as the seat of the governor:* the Hebrew here is very cryptic (literally 'to the seat of...'). The N.E.B's interpretation may be correct, though we know nothing of any 'official residence' in Jerusalem, or the point may be that Gibeon

and Mizpah were areas under the direct authority of the governor.

8. *a goldsmith...a perfumer:* there is a similar reference in verses 31–2. The very limited nature of the trades mentioned shows the partial and selective nature of this list.

9. *the district of Jerusalem:* the references here and in verse 12 are probably to the area surrounding Jerusalem, rather than to the city itself.

10. *opposite his own house:* there are several further references to local involvement of this kind. The suggestion has been made that at these points the houses concerned were actually built into the city walls, or perhaps the original wall was here beyond repair.

11. *a second section:* further evidence of the partial nature of the material is afforded by the fact that there has been no reference to a first section repaired by this group. Of seven such references to a second section, four have no mention of the first section.

12. *the help of his daughters:* an unexpected reference and one that may well be due to corruption in the text. There are many place-names here, and *daughters* often stands for dependent villages.

13–15. The district here is the same as that referred to in Nehemiah's preliminary tour of inspection (2: 13–15).

15. *the Pool of Shelah:* it is usually thought that this is an alternative spelling of the Pool of Shiloah (Isa. 8: 6; John 9: 7) and perhaps to be identified with the Lower Pool of Isa. 22: 9. If so, the description has now reached the southernmost part of the wall.

16–32. The remaining verses describe the completion of the circuit of the walls. The problems of identification, both of places and of individuals, are very similar to those noted in the first part. It is possible that future excavations may help resolve the first problem; the second is likely to remain a matter of speculation. The overall impression, however, is clear: this major work of reconstruction was regarded by succeeding generations in Jerusalem as a very considerable achievement, and the record of it was preserved, and the opportunity taken to include it as part of the total picture of restoration which Ezra–Nehemiah provides. ✻

OPPOSITION TO THE REBUILDING

4 1[a] When Sanballat heard that we were rebuilding the wall, he was very indignant; in his anger he jeered at the Jews
2 and said in front of his companions and of the garrison in Samaria, 'What do these feeble Jews think they are doing? Do they mean to reconstruct the place? Do they hope to offer sacrifice and finish the work in a day? Can they make stones again out of heaps of rubble, and burnt at
3 that?' Tobiah the Ammonite, who was beside him, said, 'Whatever it is they are building, if a fox climbs up their stone walls, it will break them down.'

4 Hear us, our God, for they treat us with contempt. Turn back their reproach upon their own heads and let them become objects of contempt in a land of captivity.
5 Do not condone their guilt or let their sin be struck off the record, for they have openly provoked the builders.

6 We built up the wall until it was continuous all round up to half its height; and the people worked with a will.
7[b] But when Sanballat and Tobiah, the Arabs and Ammonites and Ashdodites, heard that the new work on the walls of Jerusalem had made progress and that the filling of the
8 breaches had begun, they were very angry; and they all banded together to come and attack Jerusalem and to
9 create confusion. So we prayed to our God, and posted a guard day and night against them.

[a] 3: 33 *in Heb.*   [b] 4: 1 *in Heb.*

But the men of Judah said, 'The labourers' strength has 10
failed, and there is too much rubble; we shall never be
able to rebuild the wall by ourselves.' And our adver- 11
saries said, 'Before they know it or see anything, we shall
be upon them and kill them, and so put an end to the
work.' When the Jews who lived among them came in to 12
the city, they warned us many[a] times that they would
gather from every place where they lived to attack us, and 13
that they would station themselves[b] on the lowest levels
below the wall, on patches of open ground. Accordingly
I posted my people by families, armed with swords, spears,
and bows. Then I surveyed the position and at once 14
addressed the nobles, the magistrates, and all the people.
'Do not be afraid of them', I said. 'Remember the Lord,
great and terrible, and fight for your brothers, your sons
and daughters, your wives and your homes.' Our enemies 15
heard that everything was known to us, and that God had
frustrated their plans; and we all returned to our work on
the wall.

From that day forward half the men under me were 16
engaged in the actual building, while the other half stood
by holding their spears, shields, and bows, and wearing
coats of mail; and officers supervised all the people of
Judah who were engaged on the wall. The porters carry- 17
ing the loads had one hand on the load and a weapon in
the other. The builders had their swords attached to their 18
belts as they built; the trumpeter was beside me. I ad- 19
dressed the nobles, the magistrates, and all the people:

[a] *Lit.* ten.
[b] where...themselves: *so Sept.; Heb.* which you return against us and
I stationed.

'The work is great and covers much ground', I said. 'We are isolated on the wall, each man at some distance from
20 his neighbour. Wherever the trumpet sounds, rally to us
21 there, and our God will fight for us.' So we continued with the work, half the men holding the spears, from day-
22 break until the stars came out. At the same time I had said to the people, 'Let every man and his servant pass the night in Jerusalem, to act as a guard for us by night and a
23 working party by day.' So neither I nor my kinsmen nor the men under me nor my bodyguard ever took off our clothes, each keeping his right hand on[a] his weapon.

✽ No direct reference to Nehemiah has been made in ch. 3, but this next section takes up once again the story of the attempts to thwart his mission by Sanballat and his allies. There may be some suggestion also of a lack of enthusiasm among 'the men of Judah' (verse 10; and see the comment on that verse) as if to emphasize the magnitude of Nehemiah's task, and the next chapter will elaborate on these disputes within the community; but here the emphasis is on the way in which what might otherwise seem impossible can in fact be achieved by those who are protected by the divine favour.

1-3. The first reaction of Sanballat and Tobiah is one of contempt, presented so as to provide the opportunity for the prayer which follows. *the garrison in Samaria* was presumably the official Persian body of troops under the command of Sanballat as governor of the province.

4-5. Nehemiah's prayer here uses two motifs which are frequently found in the Psalms. The first is the thought that the attacks of enemies bring God's heritage into contempt, the second is the request that God will take vengeance on them. Both ideas are found, for example, in Ps. 79: 12:

[a] keeping his right hand on: *prob. rdg.; Heb. obscure.*

86

As for the contempt our neighbours pour on thee, O Lord,
  turn it back sevenfold on their own heads.

The Psalmists may well have been influenced by the particular
historical circumstances underlying their compositions, but it
is also possible that the compilers of the Nehemiah tradition
have consciously likened his circumstances to those conventionally set out in Psalms such as this.

7. The extent of the opposition is now made clearer. In
addition to the leaders already mentioned, the Arabs and
Ammonites may be regarded as those dependent on Geshem
and Tobiah respectively; the Ashdodites were the inhabitants
of the old Philistine territory, south-west of Judah, inter-
marriage with whom was to provide Nehemiah with a later
problem (13: 23).

9. *So we prayed to our God:* Nehemiah (or the writer) constantly stresses that his first response to danger is prayer.

10. The N.E.B. translators have taken this as another
editorial note indicating some doubts within the community
itself, and this may be the correct understanding. Two factors
weigh against it: the phrase translated *men of Judah* in the
Hebrew is simply 'Judah', and apparently does not refer to
any specific group, while the remainder of the verse should
probably be understood as a fragment of poetry. One is again
reminded of a Psalm of community lament, where the people
acknowledge their inability. Such a Psalm would go on to
plead for God's intervention (cp. Ps. 44: 13–16).

12–13. There are a number of difficulties in the precise
translation of these two verses, some of which are indicated
by the N.E.B. footnote. But the general sense is beyond doubt.

12. *the Jews who lived among them:* the reference here appears
to be to those sympathetic to Nehemiah who lived in territory
controlled by those who were opposing him. It may well be
that the precise legal status of the whole enterprise was far
from clear.

14. Again the reason for confidence is primarily the certainty of divine favour.

16–23. A vivid description is given of the type of precautions that were undertaken. We may feel that in various ways the measures taken might prove somewhat impractical, but the intention is clearly to further the two themes of divine favour and of the eagerness of the community to press on with its task.

23. The '*Heb. obscure*' of the N.E.B. footnote reads literally 'each his weapon the water', which was understood by the older English versions to conceal a reference to the removal of clothes for washing; the N.E.B. reading is much more likely. *

DISPUTES IN THE COMMUNITY

* At this point the account of the wall-building, which will be completed in ch. 6, is interrupted by a new theme. Apart from the ambiguous verse, 4: 10, the community has so far been presented as acting in whole-hearted unity under Nehemiah's inspiration; now, a number of economic and social issues are shown as leading to dissension and bitterness. In their present context they are used as a further apologia on behalf of Nehemiah himself, aiming to show the justice and understanding with which he governed the affairs of the community, despite the provocation under which he found himself, and it is impossible to penetrate behind this and state with confidence exactly what groups were involved or the true causes of the dissension. As the N.E.B. paragraphing indicates, there are really two parts to the chapter, one dealing with fairly specific problems, the other a more general justification of Nehemiah's methods and measures. *

ECONOMIC BURDENS

5 There came a time when the common people, both men and women, raised a great outcry against their fellow-
2 Jews. Some complained that they were giving their sons

and daughters as pledges[a] for food to keep themselves
alive; others that they were mortgaging their fields, vine- 3
yards, and houses to buy corn in the famine; others again 4
that they were borrowing money on[b] their fields and
vineyards to pay the king's tax. 'But', they said, 'our 5
bodily needs are the same as other people's, our children
are as good as theirs; yet here we are, forcing our sons
and daughters to become slaves. Some of our daughters
are already enslaved, and there is nothing we can do,
because our fields and vineyards now belong to others.' I 6
was very angry when I heard their outcry and the story
they told. I mastered my feelings and reasoned with the 7
nobles and the magistrates. I said to them, 'You are holding your fellow-Jews as pledges for debt.' I rebuked them
severely and said, 'As far as we have been able, we have 8
bought back our fellow-Jews who had been sold to other
nations; but you are now selling your own fellow-
countrymen, and they will have to be bought back by
us!' They were silent and had not a word to say. I went 9
on, 'What you are doing is wrong. You ought to live so
much in the fear of God that you are above reproach in
the eyes of the nations who are our enemies. Speaking for 10
myself, I and my kinsmen and the men under me are
advancing them money and corn. Let us give up this
taking of persons as pledges for debt. Give back today to 11
your debtors their fields and vineyards, their olive-groves
and houses, as well as the income[c] in money, and in corn,

[a] that they...as pledges: *prob. rdg.;* Heb. that they, their sons and
daughters were many.
[b] on: *so Luc. Sept.;* Heb. *om.*
[c] *Prob. rdg.;* Heb. hundredth.

12 new wine, and oil.' 'We will give them back', they
promised, 'and exact nothing more. We will do what
you say.' So, summoning the priests, I put the offenders
13 on oath to do as they had promised. Then I shook out the
fold of my robe and said, 'So may God shake out from
his house and from his property every man who does not
fulfil this promise. May he be shaken out like this and
emptied!' And all the assembled people said 'Amen' and
praised the LORD. And they did as they had promised.

* A common theme in the prophetic books is the wrongness
of members of the community losing their freedom through
economic pressure (cp. Amos 8: 4–6; Isa. 5: 8–10), and here
Nehemiah, whose work is often compared with that of a
prophet, is confronted with the same problem. As with the
prophetic condemnations, it seems likely that what is described is a situation which was constantly likely to arise in a
struggling community rather than one particular occasion.

1. *the common people...their fellow-Jews:* clearly the dispute
is within the community, but it is not possible to be more
precise and identify particular groups.

2–4. The N.E.B. has slightly altered the Hebrew text (see
N.E.B. footnote to verse 2) to set out three different com-
plaints that were being made: the need to mortgage both
their dependent relatives and their property, and the need to
borrow in order to meet their debts. If the Hebrew text is
followed, the point is rather that the number of the community made the shortage of food all the more acute.

5. The various causes of complaint are here brought together, which suggests that we should not try to differentiate
between particular groups who were affected; the problems
concerned the whole community. To be forced *to become
slaves* was regarded as a mark of deep disgrace for those who
aspired to membership of the Israelite community, though

allusions throughout the Old Testament suggest that it was not uncommon (cp. Deut. 15: 12–17).

7. *I mastered my feelings and reasoned with:* the N.E.B. translation here may be questioned. The first phrase is perhaps better translated as in the Revised Standard Version: 'I took counsel with myself'; the second is not strong enough – it is not so much reasoning with those involved as bringing charges against them that is here involved: 'I contended with. . . .' The identification of the offenders as *the nobles and the magistrates* is more specific than what has been said previously, and gives a clearer picture of some of the tensions within the community, as well as providing another link with the condemnations of the prophets (cp. Isa. 3: 11–15).

I rebuked them severely: though there is no footnote to indicate it, the N.E.B. translators here appear to have modified the Hebrew text, which makes reference to the summoning of 'a great assembly' instead of the phrase as rendered here.

8–9. An important theme developed here, and characteristic of later Jewish writings, is that malpractice not only fails to differentiate properly between Jews and others; it makes the Jews even worse than others. Paul can use similar arguments to his early converts (Rom. 2).

11. Throughout the section it is not always clear whether the abuse referred to is basically that of holding fellow-Jews as pledges for debt (so N.E.B. at verses 7 and 10) or of charging exorbitant interest on loans; the former agrees better with the issues as set out at the beginning of the chapter; the latter would fit more readily with this verse, where the point appears to be that basic possessions have been handed over to pay excessive interest-rates. Many suggestions have been made concerning the right interpretation of the word here translated *income* (see the N.E.B. footnote), but none is entirely satisfactory.

13. Stress is laid on the willingness with which the community recognized the wrongness of its way and repented

fully and freely. The obvious parallel is with the repudiation of mixed marriages in a similarly unconditional manner (Ezra 10: 12).　✻

NEHEMIAH'S GOOD EXAMPLE

14 Moreover, from the time when I was appointed governor in the land of Judah, from the twentieth to the thirty-second year of King Artaxerxes, a period of twelve years, neither I nor my kinsmen drew the governor's allowance
15 of food. Former governors had laid a heavy burden on the people, exacting from them a daily toll[a] of bread and wine to the value of forty shekels of silver. Further, the men under them had tyrannized over the people; but, for
16 fear of God, I did not behave like this. I also put all my energy into the work on this wall, and I[b] acquired no land; and all my men were gathered there for the work.
17 Also I had as guests at my table a hundred and fifty Jews, including the magistrates, as well as men who came to us
18 from the surrounding nations. The provision which had to be made each day was an ox and six prime sheep; fowls also were prepared for me, and every ten days skins[c] of wine in abundance. Yet, in spite of all this, I did not draw the governor's allowance, because the people
19 were so heavily burdened. Remember for my good, O God, all that I have done for this people.

✻ Whereas the condemnations of the first part of the chapter are very similar to those found in the prophets, it is not so common to find comparable sections to this, proclaiming the

[a] a daily toll: *prob. rdg.; Heb. obscure.*
[b] *So some MSS.; others* we.
[c] skins: *so some MSS.; others* with every kind.

individual's innocence of the charges he has brought against others. There are nevertheless links to be observed with the protestations of innocence found in many Psalms (cp. Ps. 131) or in some prophetic passages (cp. Jer. 15: 15–18).

14. *the time when I was appointed governor:* there has been no previous statement of Nehemiah's position. The tradition here seems to be somewhat at variance with that in 2: 6, where the king's questions seem to imply a short stay. The word here translated *governor* is the same as that used of the Persian 'governors' in Ezra 8: 36 and Neh. 2: 7, 9, and of Zerubbabel in Haggai (1: 1 and elsewhere). The period referred to is 445–433 B.C., if the reference is to Artaxerxes I; otherwise 384–372 B.C.

15. *Former governors:* this expression again raises problems as to Nehemiah's status. Was he one of a regular series of appointees, or is the reference here to others who had been sent on occasional special missions? The former may seem more likely, though if it is so, it becomes more difficult to understand the anger of Sanballat. It has also been suggested that someone in the king's service as 'cupbearer' (1: 11*b*) might more probably be entrusted with a particular single mission, but we do not know enough of the details of the Persian imperial service to know if this is so. The system of tolls laid upon the people by imperial officials was a customary one in the Persian Empire, and if Nehemiah really did bear all the charges involved out of his own pocket, it was a gesture both generous and costly.

19. The account of his behaviour ends characteristically with a prayer asking for his good works to be remembered. ✳

THE WALL REBUILT

When the news came to Sanballat, Tobiah, Geshem 6 the Arab, and the rest of our enemies, that I had rebuilt the wall and that not a single breach remained in it,

2 although I had not yet set up the doors in the gates, Sanballat and Geshem sent me an invitation to come and
confer with them at Hakkephirim in the plain of Ono;
3 this was a ruse on their part to do me harm. So I sent
messengers to them with this reply: 'I have important
work on my hands at the moment; I cannot come down.
Why should the work be brought to a standstill while I
4 leave it and come down to you?' They sent me a similar
invitation four times, and each time I gave them the same
5 answer. On a fifth occasion Sanballat made a similar
approach, but this time his messenger came with an open
6 letter. It ran as follows: 'It is reported among the nations
– and Gashmu[a] confirms it – that you and the Jews are
plotting rebellion, and it is for this reason that you are
rebuilding the wall, and – so the report goes – that you
7 yourself want to be king. You are also said to have put up
prophets to proclaim in Jerusalem that Judah has a king,
meaning yourself. The king will certainly hear of this. So
8 come at once and let us talk the matter over.' Here is the
reply I sent: 'No such thing as you allege has taken place;
9 you have made up the whole story.' They were all trying
to intimidate us, in the hope that we should then relax
our efforts and that the work would never be finished. So
I applied myself to it with greater energy.[b]

10   One day I went to the house of Shemaiah son of
Delaiah, son of Mehetabel, for he was confined to his
house. He said, 'Let us meet in the house of God, within
the sanctuary, and let us shut the doors, for they are
coming to kill you – they are coming to kill you by

[a] Geshem *in* 2: 19 *and* 6: 1, 2.
[b] I applied...energy: *so Sept.; Heb.* strengthen me for the work.

night.' But I said, 'Should a man like me run away? And 11
can a man like me go into the sanctuary and survive*? I
will not go in.' Then it dawned on me: God had not sent 12
him. His prophecy aimed at harming me, and Tobiah
and Sanballat had bribed him to utter it. He had been 13
bribed to frighten me into compliance and into commit-
ting sin; then they could give me a bad name and discredit
me. Remember Tobiah and Sanballat, O God, for what 14
they have done, and also the prophetess Noadiah and all
the other prophets who have tried to intimidate me.

On the twenty-fifth day of the month Elul the wall was 15
finished; it had taken fifty-two days. When our enemies 16
heard of it, and all the surrounding nations saw it,* they
thought it a very wonderful achievement,* and they
recognized that this work had been accomplished by the
help of our God.

All this time the nobles in Judah were sending many 17
letters to Tobiah, and receiving replies from him. For 18
many in Judah were in league with him, because he was a
son-in-law of Shecaniah son of Arah, and his son Jehohanan had married a daughter of Meshullam son of
Berechiah. They were always praising* him in my pre- 19
sence and repeating to him what I said. Tobiah also wrote
to me to intimidate me.

---

* As is often the case in the Chronicler's work, the description of Nehemiah's achievement is not strictly chronological.
The community disputes described in ch. 5 must have involved a period much longer than that of the rebuilding, but

[a] and survive: *or* to save his life.   [b] *Or* were afraid.
[c] they thought...achievement: *prob. rdg.; Heb.* they fell very much
in their own eyes.   [d] *Or* repeating rumours about...

now the narrative of the rebuilding is taken up again and there is stress on the divine favour which ensured that a successful completion was reached. Here also, however, it is combined with other motifs, notably the continued opposition to Nehemiah fostered by Sanballat but found also among other groups, which show even more strikingly the working of divine providence.

1. *I had rebuilt the wall:* Nehemiah should not be accused of boasting. As we have seen, the tradition of the apologia for Nehemiah stands somewhat apart from that exemplified in ch. 3, where extensive lists of wall-builders are found.

2. This is one of the many episodes in Nehemiah's career where we would very much like to know the opposition's account of events. Was this really *a ruse on their part* or was Nehemiah inordinately suspicious? If *Hakkephirim* is a place-name, it is unidentified; it may simply mean 'villages'; *the plain of Ono*, near the coast north-west of Jerusalem, was outside the area of Nehemiah's jurisdiction.

5-7. The charges here made would certainly appear to be baseless to Nehemiah and those who supported him, but again the position may have looked different to those who viewed the new situation in Jerusalem with some alarm. *rebuilding the wall* could well be construed as a bid for political independence, that is, *plotting rebellion*, and in such a bid the leader would naturally *want to be king*. The role of the prophets is instructive; they are regarded as part of the court staff, whose duties might include the proclamation *that Judah has a king*; is there some echo here of the practice in Jerusalem before the exile, when prophets may have had a part in the proclamation of a new king (cp. the role of Nathan in 1 Kings 1: 32–40)?

9. The last phrase is a free rendering of the Greek version (see N.E.B. footnote). It may be better to retain the Hebrew text and see in this concluding note another of Nehemiah's prayers, asking for divine approval of the course he has been taking.

10-14. Before reverting to the theme of the wall-building,

these verses pick up the other point made 'n the preceding section – the conspiracies against Nehemiah.

10–11. Nehemiah puts forward two reasons for not accepting the prophecy as genuine: one, that it would impugn his own courage, the other, that as a layman he could not go into the sanctuary of the temple. For these reasons, the falsity of the prophecy is apparent. One of the reasons for the decline in prophecy at this period may have been the suspicion, which was too often justified, that prophets had been hired to give a desired message, rather than speak the word of God.

10. *for he was confined to his house:* no explanation of this cryptic phrase (literally: 'and he was shut up') is given.

14. *Remember Tobiah and Sanballat:* named in this order only in this section, which seems primarily concerned with Tobiah (cp. verses 17–19). Nehemiah's prayer against his enemies is the counterpart of his appeals on his own behalf, and again has parallels in the Psalms (cp. Ps. 137: 7, where a comparable expression is found). *the prophetess Noadiah and all the other prophets:* no further details are supplied, but some antagonism between Nehemiah and the order of prophets is suggested. The only other reference to a prophetess in the work of the Chronicler is to Huldah (2 Chron. 34: 22), but it seems probable that the order of prophets regularly included some women.

15. *the month Elul:* the sixth month, that is, late Summer (August–September). *fifty-two days:* the time appears very brief, but we cannot know how extensive the necessary work was.

16. The text of this verse is very doubtful (see the N.E.B. footnote), so that the impact of this important point is somewhat weakened. But the last phrase is uncontested: the acknowledgement by the surrounding peoples of God's active providence.

18. This note about Tobiah would accord well with the suggestion that he was an ancestor of the prominent family of

later times called the Tobiads (cp. 2: 10 and the commentary there). Part of the apologia for Nehemiah may have been directed against others in Judah who were hostile to the policy he represented; there may be a link here between the antagonism implied among the nobles of Judah and the slighting references to the nobles of Tekoa in 3: 5. ✳

OFFICIALS APPOINTED: THE CENSUS RECORD

7 Now when the wall had been rebuilt, and I had set the doors in place and the gate-keepers*a* had been appointed,

2 I gave the charge of Jerusalem to my brother Hanani, and to Hananiah, the governor of the citadel, for he was trust-

3 worthy and God-fearing above other men. And I said to them, 'The entrances to Jerusalem are not to be left open during the heat of the day; the gates must be kept shut and barred while the gate-keepers are standing at ease. Appoint guards from among the inhabitants of Jerusalem, some on sentry-duty and others posted in front of their own homes.'

4   The city was large and spacious; there were few people

5 in it and no houses had yet been rebuilt. Then God prompted me to assemble the nobles, the magistrates, and the people, to be enrolled family by family. And I found the book of the genealogies of those who had been the

6*b* first to come back. This is what I found written in it: Of the captives whom Nebuchadnezzar king of Babylon had taken into exile, these are the people of the province who have returned to Jerusalem and Judah, each to his own

7 town, led by Zerubbabel, Jeshua,*c* Nehemiah, Azariah,

[a] *Prob. rdg.; Heb. adds* the singers and the Levites.
[b] *Verses 6–73: cp. Ezra 2: 1–70.*   [c] *Or* Joshua (*cp. Hag. 1: 1*).

Raamiah, Nahamani, Mordecai, Bilshan, Mispereth, Bigvai, Nehum and Baanah.

The roll of the men of the people of Israel: the family 8 of Parosh, two thousand one hundred and seventy-two; the family of Shephatiah, three hundred and seventy-two; 9 the family of Arah, six hundred and fifty-two; the family 10,11 of Pahath-moab, namely the families of Jeshua and Joab, two thousand eight hundred and eighteen; the family of 12 Elam, one thousand two hundred and fifty-four; the 13 family of Zattu, eight hundred and forty-five; the family 14 of Zaccai, seven hundred and sixty; the family of Binnui, 15 six hundred and forty-eight; the family of Bebai, six 16 hundred and twenty-eight; the family of Azgad, two 17 thousand three hundred and twenty-two; the family of 18 Adonikam, six hundred and sixty-seven; the family of 19 Bigvai, two thousand and sixty-seven; the family of Adin, 20 six hundred and fifty-five; the family of Ater, namely that 21 of Hezekiah, ninety-eight; the family of Hashum, three 22 hundred and twenty-eight; the family of Bezai, three 23 hundred and twenty-four; the family of Harif, one hun- 24 dred and twelve; the family of Gibeon, ninety-five. The 25,26 men of Bethlehem and Netophah, one hundred and eighty-eight; the men of Anathoth, one hundred and 27 twenty-eight; the men of Beth-azmoth, forty-two; the 28,29 men of Kiriath-jearim, Kephirah, and Beeroth, seven hundred and forty-three; the men of Ramah and Geba, 30 six hundred and twenty-one; the men of Michmas, one 31 hundred and twenty-two; the men of Bethel and Ai, one 32 hundred and twenty-three; the men of*a* Nebo, fifty-two; 33

[a] *Prob. rdg., cp. Ezra 2: 29; Heb. adds* the other.

34 the men[a] of the other Elam, one thousand two hundred
35 and fifty-four; the men of Harim, three hundred and
36 twenty; the men of Jericho, three hundred and forty-five;
37 the men of Lod, Hadid, and Ono, seven hundred and
38 twenty-one; the men of Senaah, three thousand nine
hundred and thirty.

39 Priests: the family of Jedaiah, of the line of Jeshua, nine
40 hundred and seventy-three; the family of Immer, one
41 thousand and fifty-two; the family of Pashhur, one thou-
42 sand two hundred and forty-seven; the family of Harim,
one thousand and seventeen.

43 Levites: the families of Jeshua and[b] Kadmiel, of the line
44 of Hodvah, seventy-four. Singers: the family of Asaph,
45 one hundred and forty-eight. Door-keepers: the family
of Shallum, the family of Ater, the family of Talmon, the
family of Akkub, the family of Hatita, and the family of
Shobai, one hundred and thirty-eight in all.

46 Temple-servitors: the family of Ziha, the family of
47 Hasupha, the family of Tabbaoth, the family of Keros,
48 the family of Sia, the family of Padon, the family of
Lebanah, the family of Hagabah, the family of Shalmai,
49 the family of Hanan, the family of Giddel, the family of
50 Gahar, the family of Reaiah, the family of Rezin, the
51 family of Nekoda, the family of Gazzam, the family of
52 Uzza, the family of Paseah, the family of Besai, the family
53 of the Meunim, the family of the Nephishesim,[c] the
family of Bakbuk, the family of Hakupha, the family of
54 Harhur, the family of Bazlith,[d] the family of Mehida,[e]

[a] *Prob. rdg.; Heb.* family (*also in verses 35–8*).
[b] and: *prob. rdg., cp. Ezra 2: 40; Heb.* to.   [c] *Or* Nephushesim.
[d] *Or* Bazluth (*cp. Ezra 2: 52*).   [e] Mehira *in some MSS.*

the family of Harsha, the family of Barkos, the family of 55
Sisera, the family of Temah, the family of Neziah, and 56
the family of Hatipha.

Descendants of Solomon's servants: the family of 57
Sotai, the family of Sophereth, the family of Perida, the 58
family of Jaalah, the family of Darkon, the family of
Giddel, the family of Shephatiah, the family of Hattil, the 59
family of Pochereth-hazzebaim, and the family of Amon.

The temple-servitors and the descendants of Solomon's 60
servants amounted to three hundred and ninety-two in
all.

The following were those who returned from Tel- 61
melah, Tel-harsha, Kerub, Addon, and Immer, but could
not establish their father's family nor whether by descent
they belonged to Israel: the family of Delaiah, the family 62
of Tobiah, the family of Nekoda, six hundred and forty-
two. Also of the priests: the family of Hobaiah, the family 63
of Hakkoz, and the family of Barzillai who had married a
daughter of Barzillai the Gileadite and went by his*a* name.
These searched for their names among those enrolled in 64
the genealogies, but they could not be found; they were
disqualified for the priesthood as unclean, and the gover- 65
nor forbade them to partake of the most sacred food until
there should be a priest able to consult the Urim and the
Thummim.

The whole assembled people numbered forty-two 66
thousand three hundred and sixty, apart from their slaves, 67
male and female, of whom there were seven thousand
three hundred and thirty-seven; and they had two hundred and forty-five singers, men and women. Their 68

[a] *Prob. rdg., cp. 1 Esdras 5: 38; Heb.* their.

horses numbered seven hundred and thirty-six, their
69 mules two hundred and forty-five,[a] their camels four
hundred and thirty-five, and their asses six thousand seven
hundred and twenty.

70   Some of the heads of families gave contributions for the
work. The governor gave to the treasury a thousand
drachmas of gold, fifty tossing-bowls, and five hundred
71 and thirty priestly robes. Some of the heads of families
gave for the fabric fund twenty thousand drachmas of
gold and two thousand two hundred minas of silver.
72 What the rest of the people gave was twenty thousand
drachmas of gold, two thousand minas of silver, and
sixty-seven priestly robes.

73a   The priests, the Levites, and some of the people lived in
Jerusalem and its suburbs;[b] the door-keepers, the singers,
the temple-servitors, and all other Israelites, lived in their
own towns.

* The greater part of this chapter consists of a list which is
substantially identical with that in Ezra 2. It is clear, however,
that it has been skilfully worked into its present context by
the editors who have used it as a natural sequel to the first
section of first-person material dealing with Nehemiah.
Some consideration is given to the nature of this list in the
comments on Ezra 2.

1. It is doubtful whether the N.E.B. is correct here in
omitting the reference to 'the singers and the Levites' (see
the footnote). At 13: 22 there is a reference to the duties of
Levites as 'guards at the gates', which is the meaning here.

2. *I gave the charge of Jerusalem:* we cannot know exactly
what is here involved, but this is a clear indication that

[a] Their horses...forty-five: *so some MSS.; others om.*
[b] in Jerusalem and its suburbs: *prob. rdg., cp.* 1 Esdras 5: 46; *Heb. om.*

Nehemiah's office was more than a simple commission affecting his own position alone. Here he has power to delegate part of his duties. *Hanani* and *Hananiah* may well be variant forms of the name of one person.

3. The N.E.B. has interpreted an obscure command in a way quite different from older versions, by taking the reference to be to the closure of the gates for a time of siesta, where other translations have taken the meaning to be that the gates should not be opened until the sun had fully risen. The N.E.B. may make better sense – it would be curious not to open gates until the sun was hot – but involves giving an unusual meaning to the Hebrew. The absence of a footnote is surprising.

5. This verse is skilfully introduced to link the theme of population in verse 4 to the census-list which follows. But if we look more closely we can see that the list with its very large numbers (verses 66–9) accords ill with the 'few people' of verse 4.

70–2. This is the only section in which significant differences exist between the two forms of the list. Possibly the references here to *contributions for the work* are intended by the editor of the list in its present form to be understood as relating to the building of the walls, whereas in Ezra 2 the reference is to the temple. ✶

The law read by Ezra and the covenant renewed

THE READING OF THE LAW

WHEN THE SEVENTH MONTH CAME, and the 73*b* Israelites were now settled in their towns, the 8 people assembled as one man in the square in front of the

Water Gate, and Ezra the scribe[a] was asked to bring the
book of the law of Moses, which the LORD had enjoined
2 upon Israel. On the first day of the seventh month, Ezra
the priest brought the law before the assembly, every man
and woman, and all who were capable of understanding
3 what they heard.[b] He read from it, facing the square in
front of the Water Gate, from early morning till noon,
in the presence of the men and the women, and those who
could understand;[c] all the people listened attentively to
4 the book of the law. Ezra the scribe stood on a wooden
platform made for the purpose,[d] and beside him stood
Mattithiah, Shema, Anaiah, Uriah, Hilkiah, and Maaseiah
on his right hand; and on his left Pedaiah, Mishael, Malchiah, Hashum, Hashbaddanah, Zechariah and Meshul-
5 lam. Ezra opened the book in the sight of all the people,
for he was standing above them; and when he opened it,
6 they all stood. Ezra blessed the LORD, the great God, and
all the people raised their hands and answered, 'Amen,
Amen'; and they bowed their heads and prostrated them-
7 selves humbly before the LORD. Jeshua, Bani, Sherebiah,
Jamin, Akkub, Shabbethai, Hodiah, Maaseiah, Kelita,
Azariah, Jozabad, Hanan, Pelaiah, the Levites,[e] expoun-
ded the law to the people while they remained in their
8 places. They read from the book of the law of God clearly,
made its sense plain and gave instruction in what was
read.

9   Then Nehemiah the governor and Ezra the priest and

[a] *Or* doctor of the law.
[b] were capable...heard: *or* would teach them to understand.
[c] could understand: *or* were to instruct.
[d] *Or* for the address.
[e] *Prob. rdg.; Heb.* and the Levites.

scribe, and the Levites who instructed the people, said to
them all, 'This day is holy to the LORD your God; do not
mourn or weep.' For all the people had been weeping
while they listened to the words of the law. Then he said 10
to them, 'You may go now; refresh yourselves with rich
food and sweet drinks, and send a share to all who cannot
provide for themselves; for this day is holy to our Lord.
Let there be no sadness, for joy in the LORD is your
strength.' The Levites silenced the people, saying, 'Be 11
quiet, for this day is holy; let there be no sadness.' So all 12
the people went away to eat and to drink, to send shares
to others and to celebrate the day with great rejoicing,
because they had understood what had been explained to
them.

On the second day the heads of families of the whole 13
people, with the priests and the Levites, assembled before
Ezra the scribe to study the law. And they found written 14
in the law that the LORD had given commandment
through Moses that the Israelites should live in arbours*a*
during the feast of the seventh month, and that they 15
should make proclamation throughout all their cities and
in Jerusalem: 'Go out into the hills and fetch branches of
olive and wild olive, myrtle and palm, and other leafy
boughs to make arbours, as prescribed.' So the people 16
went out and fetched them and made arbours for themselves, each on his own roof, and in their courts and in the
courts of the house of God, and in the square at the Water
Gate and the square at the Ephraim Gate. And the whole 17
community of those who had returned from the captivity

[a] *Or* tabernacles *or* booths.

made arbours and lived in them, a thing that the Israelites had not done from the days of Joshua[a] son of Nun to that
18 day; and there was very great rejoicing. And day by day, from the first day to the last, the book of the law of God was read. They kept the feast for seven days, and on the eighth day there was a closing ceremony, according to the rule.

* What follows is quite unexpected. The account of the work of Nehemiah is dropped, not to be taken up again until ch. 11, and instead the figure of Ezra is reintroduced. (The references to Nehemiah in 8: 9 and 10: 1 may well be glosses, and in any case are certainly not part of the same Nehemiah tradition as we have been following.) Two major questions arise with regard to this chapter: why is the material in such apparent disorder? and what can we know of the historical original of the ceremony here described?

In trying to answer the first question, the first clue must be the existence of much of this material in another form, that is, the book 1 Esdras in the Apocrypha. There, the greater part of the section here being considered (down to 8: 13*a*) is placed immediately after Ezra 10, that is to say, the Ezra material is found together without the insertion of that relating to Nehemiah. What is more difficult to decide is whether the lack of the Nehemiah material in 1 Esdras should be regarded as an omission, or whether it was inserted into our books Ezra–Nehemiah at a date after the translation of 1 Esdras. The former may perhaps be regarded as more probable; we have seen on p. 4 that there were some traditions in Judaism which venerate Ezra and ignore Nehemiah, and 1 Esdras may be one such. If this is so, then the present curious order would antedate 1 Esdras, and the answer to our problem should probably be sought along these lines.

[a] *Heb.* Jeshua.

For the Chronicler the work of restoration was to be seen as a unity. For him the maxim, 'first things first' meant, not as it might for us, a chronological order, but an order of importance. The temple must come first, then the purifying of the community, then the building of the outer walls of the city, and so finally all could reach a grand climax in the reading of the law. Neh. 8–9 could be regarded as the conclusion of the work of restoration, to which the additional material in Neh. 10–13 was merely a supplement.

The second question poses problems of a different kind. We have seen many times in the work of the Chronicler how difficult it is to penetrate behind the basic concerns of the work to discover the historical kernel, and that is certainly the case here. Behind the law-reading ceremony some have discerned the main point of Ezra's mission and have held that it must have taken place shortly after his arrival in Jerusalem, and have correlated the months listed in this chapter with those noted in Ezra 7. Others have argued that the theological concerns of the Chronicler have so overlaid this account that it is no longer possible to reconstruct the original circumstances with any confidence. Such a conclusion, though seemingly negative, at least has the merit of focusing our attention on the significance of this episode in terms of the Chronicler's own understanding of Israel's restoration; in other words, we look at what the Chronicler wanted to stress rather than read our own concerns back into the material.

One other point should be borne in mind, whatever view is taken of the problems outlined above. The biblical chronology as it stands implies that Ezra's first task had been completed for some twelve years before he proceeded to the ceremony described here. This seems so unlikely that the majority of scholars – probably rightly – have regarded the reference to Nehemiah here as a later gloss, aiming to show the two men in partnership. In other words, this should be regarded as a section dealing with Ezra, with Nehemiah having no part in it.

7: 73*b* – 8: 1. The phrasing here is modelled on that in Ezra 3: 1, at the conclusion of the first version of the list. A deliberate parallel is probably being drawn.

8: 1. *the Water Gate:* this is one of the gates referred to in the list in Neh. 3 (verse 26). *Ezra the scribe:* in verse 2 he is called 'the priest', in verse 9, 'the priest and scribe'. Both roles have been established in the first description of him in Ezra 7, and no more than a variation of emphasis appears to be intended here. *the book of the law of Moses:* in the Chronicler's presentation, we are surely meant to understand this as the Pentateuch. To attempt to establish what the book actually consisted of is much more problematic: some have seen the whole episode as a 'religious' interpretation of what was originally a 'secular' mission (cp. Ezra 7: 25f.) not involving any biblical text that we might be able to identify; others have argued that some part of the Pentateuch can be traced in *the book of the law*, but there is not enough clear evidence to enable us to reach a decision.

2. The emphasis here appears to be on the ability of the restored community to grasp the significance of the law and to put it into practice.

3. It is very doubtful whether attempts to reconstruct the extent of the law read from the time taken will be very profitable.

4–7. There is a similarity between the ceremony here described and the practice of the synagogue, known only from a later period. It is impossible to decide how far the practice here described determined later synagogue custom, and how far the description here is modelled on a practice already existing in Ezra's time. In both verses 4 and 7 thirteen names are given, and though there are some textual uncertainties, it is probably best to let this number stand, rather than attempt by emendation to get the number twelve, a number often used by the Chronicler to indicate the whole community (cp. Ezra 8: 24, 35).

8. This verse is obviously of great importance to our

understanding of the ceremony; ironically, however, what is meant by *clearly* and making the *sense plain* is neither clear nor plain. As in other parts of the work of the Chronicler (e.g. 2 Chron. 17: 7–9) the teaching function of the Levites is being stressed, but we are not sure of the exact implication. One traditional view is that the law written in Hebrew was translated into Aramaic; the beginning of the Aramaic paraphrases of the Old Testament, known as targums, was ascribed to Ezra by the later Jewish rabbis and 13: 24 might suggest that knowledge of Hebrew was imperfect by this time. Alternatively, the word translated *clearly* might imply a division into short paragraphs; the function of the Levites would then be to explain the implications of each section in turn, that is to say, something akin to 'exposition'.

9. *Nehemiah the governor:* the reference to Nehemiah is intrusive at this point (see p. 107). The word translated *governor* here is *tirshatha*, used in Ezra 2: 63 (see comment on p. 20). *do not mourn or weep:* the reaction should be seen as the proper convention rather than in emotional terms. Here, as elsewhere, there are links with the reading of the law book in the time of Josiah (2 Chron. 34).

12. No specific requirement of the law seems to be in mind here; the closest parallel is with the description of the establishment of the feast of Purim in Esther 9: 19.

13. The Greek apocryphal work, 1 Esdras, breaks off, apparently in an incomplete form, after translating part of this verse. *heads of families:* a pointer to the role which the head of the family would come to have in later Judaism in expounding the law to those for whom he was responsible.

14. The finding of Josiah's law-book had led to the keeping of Passover; on this occasion it is the autumn feast which is celebrated. The reference to what is *written in the law* is to Lev. 23: 33–6 and 39–43; here, as elsewhere, what appears to be a specific quotation is in fact a general allusion to an earlier law.

17. *the whole community:* once again the Chronicler's

emphasis on the totality of the commitment is found. All have returned; all have played their part in restoring Jerusalem; all now join in keeping festival. *from the days of Joshua the son of Nun:* this manner of saying that there had never been so great a festival since the ancient days is characteristic of the Chronicler (cp. 2 Chron. 30: 26; 35: 18). That it is not to be taken literally is clear from Ezra 3: 4. The reference to Joshua may be motivated by the idea of the restoration as a second taking possession of the holy land, the first being in the time of Joshua. ✳

FASTING AND PRAYER

✳ The greater part of ch. 9 consists of an extended prayer which sets out the past history of the people so as to underline its point – a method of presentation which is very characteristic of both Old and New Testament: it is found in several Psalms (e.g. Pss. 105 and 106), and in such New Testament passages as Stephen's speech (Acts 7) and the catalogue o heroes of faith in Heb. 11. The theological point being made is more important than any addition to our historical knowledge which may be afforded.

In the Hebrew text of this chapter no reference is made to either Ezra or Nehemiah, so that a problem is raised by its relation to other material in these books. The Greek translators resolved the problem by inserting 'And Ezra said' before the beginning of the prayer, and some English versions (e.g. the Revised Standard Version) have incorporated these words. More probably, this section was part of the material relating to the whole process of restoration available to the Chronicler and it is therefore rightly included, but it has no immediate link with either of the leaders Ezra or Nehemiah. If this is so, then one difficulty which has been felt concerning the events here described can be resolved. No mention is made of the 'day of atonement', which should have been observed according to the requirements of Lev.

16 on the tenth day of the seventh month (Lev. 23: 27). This omission, which at first sight seems surprising in view of the great importance which came to be attached to that day, may simply be due to the fact that this chapter originally had no connection with what now precedes. ✶

THE PROMISES TO THE FATHERS

On the twenty-fourth day of this month the Israelites 9 assembled for a fast, clothed in sackcloth and with earth on their heads. Those who were of Israelite descent 2 separated themselves from all the foreigners; they took their places and confessed their sins and the iniquities of their forefathers. Then they stood up in their places, and 3 the book of the law of the LORD their God was read for one fourth of the day, and for another fourth they confessed and did obeisance to the LORD their God. Upon the 4 steps assigned to the Levites stood Jeshua, Bani, Kadmiel, Shebaniah, Bunni, Sherebiah, Bani, and Kenani, and they cried aloud to the LORD their God. Then the Levites, 5 Jeshua, Kadmiel, Bani, Hashabniah, Sherebiah, Hodiah, Shebaniah, and Pethahiah, said, 'Stand up and bless the LORD your God, saying: From everlasting to everlasting thy glorious name is blessed[a] and exalted above all blessing and praise. Thou alone art the LORD; thou hast 6 made heaven, the highest heaven with all its host, the earth and all that is on it, the seas and all that is in them. Thou preservest all of them, and the host of heaven worships thee. Thou art the LORD, the God who chose Abram 7 and brought him out of Ur of the Chaldees and named

[a] thy glorious name is blessed: *prob. rdg.; Heb.* and let them bless thy glorious name.

8 him Abraham. Thou didst find him faithful to thee and didst make a covenant with him to give to him and[a] to his descendants the land of the Canaanites, the Hittites, the Amorites, the Perizzites, the Jebusites, and the Girgashites; and thou didst fulfil thy promise, for thou art just.

9 'And thou didst see the misery of our forefathers in Egypt and didst hear their cry for help at the Red Sea,[b] 10 and didst work signs and portents against Pharaoh, all his courtiers and all the people of his land, knowing how arrogantly they treated our forefathers, and thou didst 11 win for thyself a name that lives on to this day. Thou didst tear the sea apart before them so that they went through the middle of it on dry ground; but thou didst cast their pursuers into the depths, like a stone cast into 12 turbulent waters. Thou didst guide them by a pillar of cloud in the day-time and by a pillar of fire at night to give them light on the road by which they travelled. 13 Thou didst descend upon Mount Sinai and speak with them from heaven, and give them right judgements and true laws, and statutes and commandments which were 14 good, and thou didst make known to them thy holy sabbath and give them commandments, statutes, and laws 15 through thy servant Moses. Thou gavest them bread from heaven to stay their hunger and thou broughtest water out from a rock for them to quench their thirst, and thou didst bid them enter and take possession of the land which 16 thou hadst solemnly sworn to give them. But they, our forefathers, were arrogant and stubborn, and disobeyed

[a] to him and: *so Sept.; Heb. om.*
[b] *Or* the Sea of Reeds.

thy commandments. They refused to obey and did not 17
remember the miracles which thou didst accomplish
among them; they remained stubborn, and they appointed a man to lead them back to slavery in Egypt.[a] But
thou art a forgiving god, gracious and compassionate,
long-suffering and ever constant, and thou didst not
forsake them. Even when they made the image of a bull- 18
calf in metal and said, "This is your god who brought
you up from Egypt", and were guilty of great blasphemies, thou in thy great compassion didst not forsake them 19
in the wilderness. The pillar of cloud did not fail to guide
them on their journey by day nor the pillar of fire by
night to give them light on the road by which they
travelled. Thou gavest thy good spirit to instruct them; 20
thy manna thou didst not withhold from them, and thou
gavest them water to quench their thirst. Forty years long 21
thou didst sustain them in the wilderness, and they lacked
nothing; their clothes did not wear out and their feet were
not swollen.'

* The long prayer which occupies the greater part of this
and the next section makes many allusions to other biblical
passages, only some of which are noted here. In general
terms the closest links are with the point of view expressed
in the collection sometimes called the Deuteronomic history,
that is, Deuteronomy–2 Kings. Such a recital of past events
might seem inappropriate to us in prayer addressed to God,
but was in fact a characteristic feature of many Jewish prayers.
Translations have sometimes set it out in poetic form, but
it may better be regarded as a kind of stylized and rhythmic
prose.

[a] in Egypt: *so some MSS.; others* in their rebellion.

1. *a fast:* fasting as a means of acknowledging the community's sinfulness seems to have been commonly practised at this period. As well as the fasts in Ezra 8: 21 and 10: 6, there are comparable allusions elsewhere (e.g. Zech. 7: 3–5; Isa. 58: 3–7).

2. *separated themselves from all the foreigners:* once again we find the themes which are prominent all through these books, of separation, of concern for those who are to form the true people of God, and of proper descent.

3. No clear indication is given as to the relation between this ceremony and that described in ch. 8. Is this an alternative version of the same ceremony, or are particularly appropriate sections of the law now being proclaimed?

4–5. These verses provide a good example of the corruption which is liable to take place with lists of names. The two lists are clearly basically identical, but the order has been changed in one place, the same name is found in variant forms (*Shebaniah* and *Hashabniah*), and there are names which occur in one list but not the other (*Kenani, Hodiah, Pethahiah*).

5b–6. The beginning of the prayer, invoking a blessing, is characteristic of Jewish custom both in the Old Testament and later in the synagogue. Above all God is to be blessed as creator of all. In particular the wording here is reminiscent of Hezekiah's prayer at 2 Kings 19: 15, a section not used in the corresponding part of 2 Chronicles. The Chronicler's idealization of Hezekiah made the use of his prayer here especially appropriate.

7–8. The Chronicler differs from the deuteronomic writings in tracing the people's history from Abraham rather than from the exodus, and it is noteworthy that the list of tribes dispossessed is linked with the descendants of Abraham rather than with the wilderness period.

9–15. The exodus and wilderness wanderings are not passed over in silence, however, as they are in other parts of the Chronicler's work. In phrases nearly all of which represent allusions to earlier Old Testament writings (cp. e.g. verse 12 with Exod. 13: 21) the kindness of God toward his people is stressed. Other such summaries sometimes left out any reference to Mount Sinai – note the use of this name rather than 'Horeb' as in Deuteronomy (cp. Deut. 26: 5–9) – but that plays a prominent part here as the place where the commandments had been given.

16–17. As in many other Old Testament writings, the contrast is now brought out between the people who were *arrogant and stubborn, and disobeyed*, and God, who is *forgiving . . . gracious and compassionate, long-suffering and ever constant* (cp. Joel 2: 13).

18–21. God's character is shown by his continuing to act favourably toward his people despite all provocation. The reference to the guidance of God's spirit is unusual; it is somewhat reminiscent of the Psalm-like passage, Isa. 63: 11. ✲

THE PEOPLE'S CONTINUING SINFULNESS

'Thou gavest them kingdoms and peoples, allotting 22 these to them as spoils of war. Thus they took possession of the land of Sihon[a] king of Heshbon and the land of Og king of Bashan. Thou didst multiply their descendants so 23 that they became countless as the stars in the sky, bringing them into the land which thou didst promise to give to their forefathers as their possession. When their descen- 24 dants entered the land and took possession of it, thou didst subdue before them the Canaanites who inhabited it and gavest these, kings and peoples alike, into their hands to do with them whatever they wished. They captured 25 fortified cities and a fertile land and took possession of houses full of all good things, rock-hewn cisterns, vine-yards, olive-trees, and fruit-trees in abundance; so they

[a] *So one MS.; others add* and the land of.

ate and were satisfied and grew fat and found delight in
26 thy great goodness. But they were defiant and rebelled
against thee; they turned their backs on thy law and killed
thy prophets, who solemnly warned them to return to
27 thee, and they were guilty of great blasphemies. Because
of this thou didst hand them over to their enemies who
oppressed them. But when, in the time of their oppres-
sion, they cried to thee for help, thou heardest them from
heaven and in thy great compassion didst send them
28 saviours to save them from their enemies. But when they
had had a respite, they once more did what was wrong in
thine eyes; and thou didst abandon them to their enemies
who held them in subjection. But again they cried to thee
for help, and many times over thou heardest them from
29 heaven and in thy compassion didst save them. Thou
didst solemnly warn them to return to thy law, but they
grew arrogant and did not heed thy commandments; they
sinned against thy ordinances, which bring life to him
who keeps them. Stubbornly they turned away in mulish
30 obstinacy and would not obey. Many years thou wast
patient with them and didst warn them by thy spirit
through thy prophets; but they would not listen. There-
31 fore thou didst hand them over to foreign peoples. Yet in
thy great compassion thou didst not make an end of them
nor forsake them; for thou art a gracious and compassionate god.

32 'Now therefore, our God, thou great and mighty and
terrible God, who faithfully keepest covenant, do not
make light of the hardships that have befallen us – our
kings, our princes, our priests, our prophets, our forefathers, and all thy people – from the days of the kings of

Assyria to this day. In all that has befallen us thou hast 33
been just, thou hast kept faith, but we have done wrong.
Our kings, our princes, our priests, and our forefathers 34
did not keep thy law nor heed thy commandments and
the warnings which thou gavest them. Even under their 35
own kings, while they were enjoying the great prosperity
which thou gavest them and the broad and fertile land
which thou didst bestow upon them, they did not serve
thee; they did not abandon their evil ways. Today we are 36
slaves, slaves here in the land which thou gavest to our
forefathers so that they might eat its fruits and enjoy its
good things. All its produce now goes to the kings whom 37
thou hast set over us because of our sins. They have power
over our bodies, and they do as they please with our
beasts, while we are in dire distress.

'Because of all this we make a binding declaration in 38[a]
writing, and our princes, our Levites, and our priests
witness the sealing.'

* The remainder of the prayer continues in the same tone,
contrasting God's graciousness with the people's lack of
proper response. The last verses, from 32 on, are concerned
with present needs rather than a recapitulation of the past.

22–5. These verses provide a description, based mainly on
various passages in Deuteronomy, of the way in which the
LORD had led his people successfully through every crisis so
that they had inherited the promised land. Verse 25 in particular is based on the very idealized description of the land
given in Deut. 6: 11.

26–31. The same pattern of rejection by the people of the
evidence of God's kindness is continued in the description

[a] *10: 1 in Heb.*

of the period from the settlement to the exile. Verses 27f. are based on Judg. 2, especially verses 15 and 18, but the pattern there set out as characterizing the period of the judges is now applied to the whole of the people's history until the exile. The very summary and generalized form of the description of this period might be due to the fact that it has already been dealt with in 1 and 2 Chronicles, but more probably such summaries regularly took this form (cp. Ps. 106; Heb. 11); the earlier period was regarded as the formative time, and what happened later only followed well-established precedent.

32. The time *from the days of the kings of Assyria to this day* is regarded as essentially a unity: 'modern times', so to say. From this point the stress is on the need to make full acknowledgement of sin and on the plea for the continuing forbearance of God.

36. *Today we are slaves...in the land which thou gavest to our forefathers:* a sharp contrast appears here between a position of bondage and the attitude to the Persian rulers displayed elsewhere in Ezra–Nehemiah. It is a further pointer to the fact that the Chronicler is here using material from a different source, which may not even have originated in the Persian period.

37. *in dire distress:* again the picture drawn here differs markedly from the restored fortunes of the community described elsewhere. Even allowing for the formalized phraseology of ritual, a different set of circumstances appears to be envisaged.

38. As the N.E.B. footnote shows, this is the beginning of ch. 10 in the Hebrew text, and it may be regarded as an introduction to the solemn undertakings there made. At the same time it appropriately rounds off the prayer with a determination to amend the community's ways. *

COMMUNITY COMMITMENT

'Those who witness the sealing are Nehemiah the **10**
governor, son of Hacaliah, Zedekiah, Seraiah, Azariah, 2
Jeremiah, Pashhur, Amariah, Malchiah, Hattush, She- 3, 4
baniah,[a] Malluch, Harim, Meremoth, Obadiah, Daniel, 5, 6
Ginnethon, Baruch, Meshullam, Abiah, Mijamin, Maaz- 7, 8
iah, Bilgai, Shemaiah; these are the priests. The Levites: 9
Jeshua[b] son of Azaniah, Binnui of the family of Henadad,
Kadmiel; and their brethren, Shebaniah, Hodiah,[c] Kelita, 10
Pelaiah, Hanan, Mica, Rehob, Hashabiah, Zaccur, 11, 12
Sherebiah, Shebaniah, Hodiah, Bani, Beninu.[d] The chiefs 13, 14
of the people: Parosh, Pahath-moab, Elam, Zattu, Bani,
Bunni, Azgad, Bebai, Adonijah, Bigvai, Adin, Ater, 15,16,17
Hezekiah, Azzur, Hodiah, Hashum, Bezai, Hariph, 18, 19
Anathoth, Nebai,[e] Magpiash, Meshullam, Hezir, Meshe- 20, 21
zabel, Zadok, Jaddua, Pelatiah, Hanan, Anaiah, Hoshea, 22, 23
Hananiah, Hasshub, Hallohesh, Pilha, Shobek, Rehum, 24, 25
Hashabnah, Maaseiah, Ahiah, Hanan, Anan, Malluch, 26, 27
Harim, Baanah.

'The rest of the people, the priests, the Levites, the 28
door-keepers, the singers, the temple-servitors, with their
wives, their sons, and their daughters, all who are capable
of understanding, all who for the sake of the law of God
have kept themselves apart from the foreign population,
join with the leading brethren,[f] when the oath is put to 29

[a] *Or, with some MSS.,* Shecaniah.
[b] *Prob. rdg.; Heb.* and Jeshua.
[c] *Or, with Ezra 2: 40,* Hodaviah.
[d] *Or, with slight change,* Kenani, *cp. 9: 4.*
[e] *Or* Nobai.
[f] the leading brethren: *prob. rdg.; Heb.* their brethren, their leading
men.

them, in swearing to obey God's law given by Moses the servant of God, and to observe and fulfil all the commandments of the LORD our Lord, his rules and his statutes.

30 'We will not give our daughters in marriage to the foreign population or take their daughters for our sons.

31 If on the sabbath these people bring in merchandise, especially corn, for sale, we will not buy from them on the sabbath or on any holy day. We will forgo the crops of the seventh year and release every person still held as a pledge for debt.

32 'We hereby undertake the duty of giving yearly the third of a shekel for the service of the house of our God,

33 for the Bread of the Presence, the regular grain-offering and whole-offering, the sabbaths, the new moons, the appointed seasons, the holy-gifts, and the sin-offerings to make expiation on behalf of Israel, and for all else that has

34 to be done in the house of our God. We, the priests, the Levites, and the people, have cast lots for the wood-offering, so that it may be brought into the house of our God by each family in turn, at appointed times, year by year, to burn upon the altar of the LORD our God, as

35 prescribed in the law. We undertake to bring the first-fruits of our land and the firstfruits of every fruit-tree,

36 year by year, to the house of the LORD; also to bring to the house of our God, to the priests who minister in the house of our God, the first-born of our sons and of our cattle, as prescribed in the law, and the first-born of our

37 herds and of our flocks; and to bring to the priests the first kneading of our dough,*a* and the first of the fruit of every tree, of the new wine and of the oil, to the store-

[a] *So Sept.; Heb. adds* and our contributions.

rooms in the house of our God; and to bring to the Levites the tithes from our land, for it is the Levites who collect the tithes in all our farming villages. The Aaronite priest 38 shall be with the Levites when they collect the tithes; and the Levites shall bring up one tenth of the tithes to the house of our God, to the appropriate rooms in the store-house. For the Israelites and the Levites shall bring the 39 contribution of corn, new wine, and oil to the rooms where the vessels of the sanctuary are kept, and where the ministering priests, the door-keepers, and the singers are lodged. We will not neglect the house of our God.'

* Like its predecessors, this chapter presents problems with regard to its original context. As it stands, it is a sequel to the prayer in ch. 9, but the connection is really a tenuous one, and unlikely to have been original. Nor is the connection with Nehemiah suggested by the mention of his name in verse 1 likely to be original; as in 8: 9 it is probably a gloss. What we have here is part of the total picture of restoration, evidenced this time by the commitment to which the com-munity bound itself in respect of separation from aliens, sabbath-observance, and the proper maintenance of the temple and its worship. All these were themes of sufficient import-ance to the Chronicler to be included within his work and associated with Ezra and Nehemiah; but it is unlikely that the particular ceremony here described originally related to either of them.

1. *Those who witness the sealing:* we have no indication of the form of the ceremony. The word 'covenant' has some-times been used in connection with it, but the actual term does not appear. *Nehemiah the governor:* as in 8: 9, probably a gloss. The same word for governor, *tirshatha*, is used as there.

1–27. The list is in the by now familiar order of *priests*, *Levites* and lay-people (*chiefs of the people*). The lists here are independent of the many other lists in the Chronicler's work, but parts of them show connections with those found elsewhere. Thus the names of the priests in verses 1–8 have links with the lists in Neh. 12: 2–7 and 12–21; the Levites in verses 9–13 have many names in common with the Levitical lists in Neh. 12: 8–9 and 24–5; while the names of lay-people have most links with the long list in Ezra 2 and Neh. 7, though many names here are not found there. The history of the tradition underlying these lists is a complex one which cannot now be unravelled with confidence.

28. The order of groups in this verse is curious. It may be better to understand 'the rest of the people, that is, the priests, the Levites ...'; this covers all those not listed in verses 1–27. *all who for the sake of the law ... foreign populations:* the note of exclusiveness is found again, and here it is put in terms which make it clear that any idea of a distinct 'people of God' must involve some measure of such exclusiveness. The demand of *the law of God* involves such a response.

29. The manner in which this verse is expressed hardly seems to fit with the ceremony just described; some other comparable occasion may be in mind here, which is then elaborated in the form of the oaths which follow.

30–9. An interesting parallel to the ceremony here described has been found among the Dead Sea Scrolls from Qumran. The document known as the Community Rule lays down requirements for entry into the community, with special liturgical functions for priests and Levites, in setting out God's graciousness to his people and acknowledging the people's failure to respond. The ceremony ends, as in the present context, with solemn undertakings entered into by all those present.

30. The theme of Ezra 10 and Neh. 13 comes first; the oath not to allow the daughters of the community to be given in marriage to foreigners goes a step further than the other

passages, except Ezra 9: 12; elsewhere the concern is with the marrying of foreign women.

31. Sabbath observance was a major concern of the community in later Old Testament times, and the concern here is similar to that described in Neh. 13: 13-22. The other promises here are not matters that occur in any narrative context in these books; those with regard to *the seventh year* may be directly based on the requirements of the Pentateuch (Lev. 25).

32. *the third of a shekel:* no command of this nature has survived in the Old Testament, and we cannot be certain whether it was an established custom or whether the Chronicler was anxious to encourage generosity toward the temple. At a later date a half-shekel tax was required (Matt. 17: 24; see the Revised Standard Version).

33. The list here summarizes the basic ritual requirements of the Pentateuch in regard to the temple. Whereas other parts of the Chronicler's work have shown links of a close nature with Deuteronomy, the basis of what is set out here is to be found in the Priestly material in Numbers. The Chronicler is really the heir to both traditions.

34. *the wood-offering:* not mentioned in the Pentateuch, perhaps because it would be illogical to do so in a context conventionally identified with the wilderness. The theme is picked up again at the very end of the book (Neh. 13: 31).

35-7. The pledges concerning *firstfruits* and *first-born* are again based on the Pentateuch, this time a variety of passages in Exodus and Numbers (cp. Exod. 13: 2; Num. 18: 12-16).

37. *to bring to the Levites the tithes:* this requirement is found in the Pentateuch, but not that which places upon the Levites the responsibility of collecting the tithes. The last section of the chapter elaborates on the mechanics of the bringing of the offerings.

39. *We will not neglect the house of our God:* it seems most probable that at this point we hear the Chronicler, both describing what had taken place according to tradition at

some point in the past and also exhorting his contemporaries to similar diligence. The whole of this section provides a statement in brief of what he regarded as the appropriate attitude to the now-restored temple. ✳

THE REGISTER OF THE COMMUNITY

11 The leaders of the people settled in Jerusalem; and the rest of the people cast lots to bring one in every ten to live in Jerusalem, the holy city, while the remaining nine lived
2 in other towns. And the people were grateful to all those who volunteered to live in Jerusalem.

3 These are the chiefs of the province who lived in Jerusalem; but, in the towns of Judah, other Israelites, priests, Levites, temple-servitors, and descendants of Solomon's servants lived on their own property, in their
4 own towns. Some members of the tribes of Judah and Benjamin lived in Jerusalem. Of Judah: Athaiah son of Uzziah, son of Zechariah, son of Amariah, son of Shep-
6 hatiah, son of Mahalalel of the family of Perez, all of whose family, to the number of four hundred and sixty-
5 eight men of substance, lived in Jerusalem; and Maaseiah son of Baruch, son of Col-hozeh, son of Hazaiah, son of Adaiah, son of Joiarib, son of Zechariah of the Shelanite family.

7 These were the Benjamites: Sallu son of Meshullam, son of Joed, son of Pedaiah, son of Kolaiah, son of
8 Maaseiah, son of Ithiel, son of Isaiah, and his kinsmen[a] Gabbai and Sallai,[b] nine hundred and twenty-eight in all.

[a] his kinsmen: *so Luc. Sept.; Heb.* after him.
[b] Gabbai and Sallai: *these names are uncertain.*

Joel son of Zichri was their overseer, and Judah son of 9
Hassenuah was second over the city.[a]

Of the priests: Jedaiah son of Joiarib, son of[b] Seraiah, 10,11
son of Hilkiah, son of Meshullam, son of Zadok, son of
Meraioth, son of Ahitub, supervisor of the house of God,
and his[c] brethren responsible for the work in the temple, 12
eight hundred and twenty-two in all; and Adaiah son of
Jeroham, son of Pelaliah, son of Amzi, son of Zechariah,
son of Pashhur, son of Malchiah, and his brethren, heads 13
of fathers' houses, two hundred and forty-two in all; and
Amasai[d] son of Azarel, son of Ahzai, son of Meshillemoth,
son of Immer, and his[e] brethren, men of substance, a 14
hundred and twenty-eight in all; their overseer was
Zabdiel son of Haggedolim.

And of the Levites: Shemaiah son of Hasshub, son of 15
Azrikam, son of Hashabiah, son of Bunni; and Shab- 16
bethai and Jozabad of the chiefs of the Levites, who had
charge of the external business of the house of God; and 17
Mattaniah son of Micah, son of Zabdi,[f] son of Asaph,
who as precentor led the prayer of thanksgiving,[g] and
Bakbukiah who held the second place among his brethren; and Abda son of Shammua, son of Galal, son of
Jeduthun. The number of Levites in the holy city was 18
two hundred and eighty-four in all.

The gate-keepers who kept guard at the gates were 19
Akkub, Talmon, and their brethren, a hundred and

[a] second over the city: *or* over the second quarter of the city.
[b] son of: *prob. rdg.; Heb. obscure.*
[c] *Prob. rdg.; Heb.* their.
[d] *Prob. rdg.; Heb.* Amashsai.
[e] *So Sept.; Heb.* their.   [f] *Or, with Luc. Sept.,* Zichri.
[g] as precentor...thanksgiving: *mng. uncertain.*

20 seventy-two. The rest of the Israelites[a] were in all the towns of Judah, each man on his own inherited property.

21 But the temple-servitors lodged on Ophel, and Ziha and Gishpa were in charge of them.

22 The overseer of the Levites in Jerusalem was Uzzi son of Bani, son of Hashabiah, son of Mattaniah, son of Mica, of the family of Asaph the singers, for the supervision of

23 the business of the house of God. For they were under the king's orders, and there was obligatory duty for the

24 singers every day. Pethahiah son of Meshezabel, of the family of Zerah son of Judah, was the king's adviser on all matters affecting the people.

25 As for the hamlets with their surrounding fields: some of the men of Judah lived in Kiriath-arba and its villages, in Dibon and its villages, and in Jekabzeel[b] and its ham-

26,27 lets, in Jeshua, Moladah, and Bethpelet, in Hazar-shual

28 and in Beersheba and its villages, in Ziklag and in Meco-

29 nah and its villages, in Enrimmon, Zorah, and Jarmuth,

30 in Zanoah, Adullam, and their hamlets, in Lachish and its fields and Azekah and its villages. Thus they occupied the country from Beersheba to the Valley of Hinnom.

31 The men of Benjamin lived in[c] Geba, Michmash, Aiah,

32 and Bethel with its villages, in Anathoth, Nob, and

33,34 Ananiah, in Hazor, Ramah, and Gittaim, in Hadid,

35 Zeboim, and Neballat, in Lod, Ono, and[d] Geharashim.[e]

36 And certain divisions of the Levites in Judah were attached to Benjamin.

[a] *Prob. rdg.; Heb. adds* the levitical priests.
[b] Kabzeel *in 1 Chr. 11: 22.*   [c] *Prob. rdg.; Heb.* from.
[d] and: *prob. rdg.; Heb. om.*
[e] *Or* and the Valley of Woods *or* and the Valley of Craftsmen.

* There is a sense in which the remainder of the work can be regarded as an appendix, even though each chapter contains sections deriving from the first-person Nehemiah material. The essential work of restoring the city, its temple, its walls and its community has been described, and no major new themes remain to be introduced. But we have seen that the Chronicler likes to include a fuller selection of the material available to him than is strictly necessary, and so these last chapters illustrate the themes already set out – in particular the membership of the new community and the maintenance of its purity. Ezra is not again mentioned, save for a note at 12: 36, which is probably a later addition; the Nehemiah sections are not closely related to their context; and to a much greater extent than the earlier part of the work these last three chapters consist of fragmentary episodes the relation of which to one another is quite problematic.

1–2. The theme of tithing at the end of ch. 10 may provide the link to this note, where the people are as it were 'tithed' for the privilege of living in Jerusalem. The theme is the same as that of 7: 4–5, but there is no obvious connection with that passage.

3–24. Instead of a list of those involved, we now find a variety of extracts of census material, part of which has already been used by the Chronicler. In particular the material here is very close to that found in 1 Chron. 9: 2–34. It is always difficult to decide which of two forms of a list of names is the earlier, but it is generally agreed that this material antedates the form found in 1 Chronicles.

4. In the corresponding section in 1 Chron. 9, reference is here made to 'men of Ephraim and Manasseh' (verse 3); no such reference is found anywhere in Ezra–Nehemiah.

11. Again this verse affords an interesting basis for comparison with other material, this time of a genealogical nature. The family tree of Seraiah is a variant of that already found in 1 Chron. 6: 1–15 and 9 and Ezra 7. The N.E.B rendering here is different from that of other English versions,

which have followed the Hebrew more closely by seeing another proper name, 'Jachin', between *Joiarib* and *Seraiah*.

25–36. These verses give an indication of the extent of the area covered by the Jerusalem jurisdiction. These lists have no direct literary relationship to any other known to us, though there are similarities with the 'city-lists' in Josh. 15. The area covered is a very limited one, smaller in extent than the kingdom of Judah before the exile. In this section the 'all Israel' theme is not present; instead the emphasis is entirely upon Judah and Benjamin. ✳

GENEALOGIES OF PRIESTS AND LEVITES

12 These are the priests and the Levites who came back with Zerubbabel son of Shealtiel, and Jeshua:[a] Seraiah,
2,3 Jeremiah, Ezra, Amariah, Malluch, Hattush, Shecaniah,
4,5 Rehum, Meremoth, Iddo, Ginnethon,[b] Abiah, Mijamin,
6,7 Maadiah, Bilgah, Shemaiah, Joiarib, Jedaiah, Sallu, Amok, Hilkiah, Jedaiah. These were the chiefs of the priests and of their brethren in the days of Jeshua.

8 And the Levites: Jeshua, Binnui, Kadmiel, Sherebiah, Judah, and Mattaniah, who with his brethren was in
9 charge of the songs of thanksgiving. And Bakbukiah and Unni their brethren stood opposite them in the service.
10 And Jeshua was the father of Joiakim, Joiakim the father
11 of Eliashib, Eliashib of Joiada, Joiada the father of Jona-
12 than,[c] and Jonathan the father of Jaddua. And in the days of Joiakim the priests who were heads of families were:
13 of Seraiah, Meraiah; of Jeremiah, Hananiah; of Ezra,
14 Meshullam; of Amariah, Jehohanan; of Malluch,[d]
15 Jonathan; of Shebaniah, Joseph; of Harim, Adna; of

[a] Or Joshua.
[b] *So many MSS.; others* Ginnethoi.
[c] Johanan *in verse 22.*
[d] *Prob. rdg.; Heb.* Malluchi, *or* Melichu.

Meraioth,[a] Helkai; of Iddo, Zechariah; of Ginnethon, 16
Meshullam; of Abiah, Zichri; of Miniamin[b]; of Moadiah, 17
Piltai; of Bilgah, Shammua; of Shemaiah, Jehonathan; of 18,19
Joiarib, Mattenai; of Jedaiah, Uzzi; of Sallu,[c] Kallai; of 20
Amok, Eber; of Hilkiah, Hashabiah; of Jedaiah, Netha- 21
neel.

[d]The heads of the priestly families[e] in the days of 22
Eliashib, Joiada, Johanan, and Jaddua were recorded down
to[f] the reign of Darius the Persian. The heads of the 23
levitical families were recorded in the annals only down
to the days of Johanan the grandson[g] of Eliashib. And the 24
chiefs of the Levites: Hashabiah, Sherebiah, Jeshua,
Binnui,[h] Kadmiel, with their brethren in the other turn
of duty, to praise and to give thanks, according to the
commandment of David the man of God, turn by turn,
Mattaniah, Bakbukiah, Obadiah, Meshullam, Talmon. 25
and Akkub were gate-keepers standing guard at the gate-
houses. This was the arrangement in the days of Joiakim 26
son of Jeshua, son of Jozadak, and in the days of Nehemiah the governor and of Ezra the priest and scribe.

* This last genealogical section is concerned with the priestly
families and the Levites. Some of it has been used already in
a slightly variant form, but other parts are of interest in that
they bring us down to a date significantly later than the rest

[a] Meremoth *in Luc. Sept. (cp. verse 3).*
[b] *A name is missing here.*
[c] *Prob. rdg., cp. verse 7; Heb.* Sallai.
[d] *Prob. rdg.; Heb. prefixes* The Levites.
[e] heads...families: *prob. rdg.; Heb.* heads of the families and the priests.
[f] down to: *so many MSS.; others* upon.
[g] *Lit.* son.
[h] Jeshua, Binnui: *prob. rdg.; Heb.* and Jeshua son of.

of these books (see on verse 22). This may suggest that some of this section was added after the main body of the work had been completed, or it may provide an indication of the approximate date of the Chronicler himself.

1–7. Twenty-two names are here listed; all but one (*Hattush*) reappear in verses 12–21, sometimes in slightly variant forms. (The N.E.B. has sometimes harmonized these variants and sometimes left them; see footnotes.) There are also connections with the list in 10: 2–8, the parallel ending with *Shemaiah*. The Hebrew text suggests that the names from *Joiarib* to *Jedaiah* are an addition to the basic list, but this does not appear in N.E.B. As presented here, the list is alleged to be of those who returned in the sixth century, but basically the same list in its other forms is presented in quite different historical contexts and we have no means of establishing its origin.

8–9. The heading in verse 1 would suggest that the Levites here should be grouped with the priests of verses 1–7; but the N.E.B. has taken them as separate, because the note about their position during the service suggests a different origin for these names.

10–11. A different, 'family-tree' type of list traces the succession of high priests; this is not specifically stated, but the intention seems clear. Scholars have frequently accepted it in the terms set out in N.E.B., as giving details of six direct descendants. But since Jeshua was active about 520 B.C., and Jaddua was said to have been alive at the time of Alexander the Great, that is, about 330 B.C., according to a story in the Jewish historian, Josephus (*Antiquities*, XI, 297–347), such a simple solution is most improbable. The high priest would not have been appointed before he reached a mature age, and an average incumbency of more than thirty years is scarcely credible. Either a number of names have been omitted, or the tradition which makes Jaddua a contemporary of Alexander should be rejected; Josephus is often extremely confused in his chronology. Of the individual names, Eliashib is probably the high priest mentioned in 3: 1, but as was indicated there, there is no certain basis for making him a contemporary of Nehemiah. Jonathan is commonly taken to be a scribal error for 'Johanan' who appears at the corresponding place in the list of verse 22; this may be right, though it is dangerously easy to smooth out discrepancies of this kind by supposing scribal errors to have taken place.

12–21. As already indicated, the family names here are substantially those of verses 1–7, with details added as to the *heads of families* at the time of Joiakim (perhaps some time in the first half of the fifth century B.C.).

22. The significance of this verse is apparently to stress that records concerning the priestly families were maintained during the high-priesthood of those mentioned. It is noteworthy that *Johanan* is found here and in the next verse as against the 'Jonathan' of verse 11. *the reign of Darius the Persian:* there were three Persian kings so named. Darius I, mentioned in Ezra 4–6, who reigned 522–486 B.C., could only be relevant here if the Hebrew preposition rendered *down to* is instead translated 'from', in which case the reference would be to his reign as the time when such records were first available. Otherwise the reference must be to either Darius II (423–404), or, if Josephus' testimony concerning Jaddua is accepted, Darius III (336–330), the last Persian king and opponent of Alexander.

23. *Johanan the grandson of Eliashib:* the N.E.B. has modified the meaning here as in Ezra 10: 6. In each case it may be a right interpretation, but we should be warned of the variety of shifts that must be adopted in order to achieve a smooth historical sequence from the material available.

24–5. As elsewhere the material relating to Levites is less in quantity than, and different in origin from, that for the priests.

26. This verse appears as a harmonizing conclusion, linking the very disparate material which has been used to its present context, and implying that Joiakim, Nehemiah and

Ezra were all contemporary with one another. Historically, such a conclusion is unlikely; its justification must be sought in the Chronicler's conviction that the restoration of the holy community in the holy city was essentially one divinely-guided act. ✻

THE DEDICATION OF THE WALL

27 At the dedication of the wall of Jerusalem they sought out the Levites in all their settlements, and brought them to Jerusalem to celebrate the dedication with*a* rejoicing, with thanksgiving and song, to the accompaniment of
28 cymbals, lutes, and harps. And the Levites,*b* the singers, were assembled from*c* the district round Jerusalem and
29 from the hamlets of the Netophathites; also from Beth-gilgal and from the region of Geba and Beth-azmoth;*d* for the singers had built themselves hamlets in the neigh-
30 bourhood of Jerusalem. The priests and the Levites puri-fied themselves; and they purified the people, the gates,
31 and the wall. Then I brought the leading men of Judah up on to the city wall, and appointed two great choirs to give thanks. One went in procession*e* to the right, going
32 along the wall to the Dung Gate; and after it went
33 Hoshaiah with half the leading men of Judah, and
34 Azariah, Ezra, Meshullam, Judah, Benjamin, Shemaiah,
35 and Jeremiah; and certain of the priests with trumpets: Zechariah son of Jonathan, son of Shemaiah, son of Mattanaiah, son of Micaiah, son of Zaccur, son of Asaph,

[a] *Prob. rdg.; Heb.* and.
[b] the Levites: *prob. rdg.; Heb.* the sons of.
[c] *So Luc. Sept.; Heb.* and from.
[d] Beth-azmoth: *prob. rdg., cp. 7: 28; Heb.* Azmoth.
[e] One...procession: *prob. rdg.; Heb.* Processions.

and his kinsmen, Shemaiah, Azarel, Milalai, Gilalai, Maai, 36
Nethaneel, Judah, and Hanani, with the musical instru-
ments of David the man of God; and Ezra the scribe led
them. They went past the Fountain Gate and thence 37
straight forward by the steps up to the City of David, by
the ascent to the city wall, past the house of David, and
on to the Water Gate on the east. The other thanksgiving 38
choir went to the left,[a] and I followed it with half the
leading men of[b] the people, continuing along the wall,
past the Tower of the Ovens[c] to the Broad Wall, and past 39
the Ephraim Gate, and over the Jeshanah Gate,[d] and over
the Fish Gate, taking in the Tower of Hananel and the
Tower of the Hundred, as far as the Sheep Gate; and they
halted at the Gate of the Guardhouse. So the two thanks- 40
giving choirs took their place in the house of God, and I
and half the magistrates with me; and the priests Eliakim, 41
Maaseiah, Miniamin, Micaiah, Elioenai, Zechariah, and
Hananiah, with trumpets; and Maaseiah, Shemaiah, 42
Eleazar, Uzzi, Jehohanan, Malchiah, Elam, and Ezer. The
singers, led by Izrahiah, raised their voices. A great 43
sacrifice was celebrated that day, and they all rejoiced
because God had given them great cause for rejoicing;
the women and children rejoiced with them. And the
rejoicing in Jerusalem was heard a long way off.

On that day men were appointed to take charge of the 44
store-rooms for the contributions, the firstfruits, and the
tithes, to gather in the portions required by the law for

[a] to the left: *prob. rdg.; Heb.* to the front.
[b] the leading men of: *prob. rdg.; Heb. om.*
[c] *Or* Furnaces.
[d] the Jeshanah Gate: *or* the gate of the Old City.

the priests and Levites according to the extent of the farm-
lands round the towns; for all Judah was full of rejoicing
45 at the ministry of the priests and Levites. And they performed the service of their God and the service of purification, as did the singers and the door-keepers, according
to the rules laid down by David and[a] his son Solomon.
46 For it was in the days of David that Asaph took the lead
as chief of the singers and director[b] of praise and thanks-
47 giving to God. And in the days of Zerubbabel and of
Nehemiah all Israel gave the portions for the singers and
the door-keepers as each day required; and they set apart
the portion for the Levites, and the Levites set apart the
portion for the Aaronites.

✶ This section can be divided into two: the main part, which
includes more first-person Nehemiah material, is concerned
with the dedication ceremony; appended to it is a note
dealing with the organization of priestly duties. (The section
13: 1–3 might also appropriately be grouped with this
material, but the sub-heading in N.E.B. has linked it rather
with what follows.) The picture of the dedication is clearly
for the most part a ritual procession upon the walls; our
knowledge is again limited by the fact that the places named
are not known to us.

27–30. These verses are not part of the first-person material
and present a kind of summary of the occasion, with special
emphasis on the role of Levites and singers. The Netophathites came from Netophah, apparently near Bethlehem (cp.
Ezra 2: 22), and are frequently mentioned in the Chronicler's
work (cp. 1 Chron. 2: 54; 11: 30).

31–43. This section portrays Nehemiah in a more promi-

[a] *So many MSS.; others om.*
[b] *Prob. rdg.; Heb.* song.

nent role in religious matters than the earlier first-person material. The picture given by the N.E.B. translation is of two processions, each proceeding around half of the wall, and though this involves some emendation of the Hebrew text (see footnotes), it is probably the right interpretation. No indication is given of the relation between the events described here and the actual completion of the wall-building in ch. 6, of which this appears to be either a sequel or an alternative account.

32–6. For the most part the names listed here are found elsewhere, but not as a list, and there are no grounds for identifying any particular individuals. The 'family-tree' genealogy of Zechariah is unexpected; it does not accord with any other list of the family of Asaph, who played a leading part in the music of the second temple (cp. 1 Chron. 25).

36. *and Ezra the scribe led them*: another harmonizing note, part of the editorial process which stresses both the prominence of Ezra in all religious affairs and the fact that the two leaders were contemporaries.

40. The order of verses appears to be misplaced at this point; the arrival *in the house of God* being described before the composition of the other party, the make-up of which corresponds with that of the first group.

43. *the rejoicing in Jerusalem was heard a long way off*: this verse, which can be regarded as the end of Nehemiah's first mission, corresponds in many ways to Ezra 3: 13. In both cases the sound of joy was *heard a long way off*; there because the work of restoration had begun once more, here because it had now been brought to a triumphant conclusion.

44. *On that day*: need not be taken literally. The phrase could mean 'in that period' or even, as probably here, be a mere link between two separate pieces of material. The same is true of 13: 1. The note appears to come from the Chronicler as an indication of the establishment of the detailed forms of service in the second temple on the pattern of the first.

47. *in the days of Zerubbabel and of Nehemiah:* what may originally have been intended as an inclusive reference, from Zerubbabel to Nehemiah, has come to be presented as if the two were contemporaries. We see here the beginning of the chronological confusion which led to the tradition in 2 Macc. 1: 18 of Nehemiah as the restorer of the city on the first return from exile. Both of them are given a religious role which in other forms of the tradition would be ascribed to Jeshua and Ezra. *Aaronites:* as throughout the work of the Chronicler, it is assumed that the priests are those who can establish descent from Aaron. ✴

Nehemiah's reforms

✴ The work ends with an account of various actions of Nehemiah, aptly described by the N.E.B. heading as his reforms, though the section might better be held to begin with verse 4. Though the actions are separate, they all have a common concern for the preservation of the purity now safely re-established. The danger in this situation comes partly from internal weakness, whereby the community failed to live up to its responsibilities, and partly from foreign pressure and infiltration. Nehemiah is represented as being equally determined to stamp out each source of weakness. After verses 1-3, the chapter consists of first-person material. ✴

RENEWED OPPOSITION TO NEHEMIAH

13 ON THAT DAY at the public reading from the book of Moses, it was found to be laid down that no Ammonite or Moabite should ever enter the assembly of
2 God, because they did not meet the Israelites with food and water but hired Balaam to curse them, though our

God turned the curse into a blessing. When the people 3
heard the law, they separated from Israel all who were of
mixed blood.

But before this, Eliashib the priest, who was appointed 4
over the store-rooms of the house of our God, and who
was connected by marriage with Tobiah, had provided 5
for his use a large room where formerly they had kept the
grain-offering, the incense, the temple vessels, the tithes
of corn, new wine, and oil prescribed for the Levites,
singers, and door-keepers, and the contributions for the
priests. All this time I was not in Jerusalem because, in the 6
thirty-second year of Artaxerxes king of Babylon, I had
gone to the king. Some time later, I asked permission
from him and returned to Jerusalem. There I discovered 7
the wicked thing that Eliashib had done for Tobiah's sake
in providing him with a room in the courts of the house
of God. I was greatly displeased and threw all Tobiah's 8
belongings out of the room. Then I gave orders that the 9
room should be purified, and that the vessels of the house
of God, with the grain-offering and incense, should be
put back into it.

I also learnt that the Levites had not been given their 10
portions; both they and the singers, who were responsible
for their respective duties, had made off to their farms. So 11
I remonstrated with the magistrates and said, 'Why is
the house of God deserted?' And I recalled the men and
restored them to their places. Then all Judah brought the 12
tithes of corn, new wine, and oil into the storehouses; and 13
I put in charge of them Shelemiah the priest, Zadok the
accountant, and Pedaiah a Levite, with Hanan son of
Zaccur, son of Mattaniah, as their assistant, for they were

considered trustworthy men; their duty was the distribu-
14 tion of their shares to their brethren. Remember this, O
God, to my credit, and do not wipe out of thy memory
the devotion which I have shown in the house of my God
and in his service.

* The first three verses really belong with what precedes,
the form being parallel to that of 12: 44–7. The section seems
like another account of the action taken in regard to mixed
marriages, alongside that recorded in Ezra 10, and Nehemiah's
own action later in this chapter. The remainder of the section
illustrates the continuing opposition within influential
strata of the community to Nehemiah and the course of
action he was pursuing.

1. *the public reading from the book of Moses:* it appears that a
regular ceremony is here being described, as against the once-
for-all occasion of ch. 8. The passage referred to is Deut.
23: 3–6, where the hostile reference to Balaam is already
found.

3. The separation is here recorded without comment; both
the other accounts have been elaborated so as to emphasize
the part played by Ezra or by Nehemiah.

4. *Eliashib the priest:* doubts have been expressed whether
this is the same Eliashib as the person mentioned in 3: 1 and
12: 11, 22, on the grounds that the high priest would not be
described as *appointed over the store-rooms.* It is doubtful if
there is much force in this argument, since we know little of
the detailed arrangements and titles of the period, and it
certainly seems as if the Chronicler intended his readers to
take the various references as being to only one man.

connected by marriage with Tobiah: this phrase, and the whole
episode, sheds considerable light on the relations between
Nehemiah and his opponents. They cannot be regarded
simply as foreigners, or as political intriguers, but they clearly
enjoyed considerable status within the Jerusalem community.

Possibly, one purpose of the Nehemiah material is to justify the action which he had taken, which may well have involved him in considerable unpopularity at the time. The reference to Tobiah might lend support to the view that there was a link with the later Tobiad family (cp. the note on 2: 10).

6. The chronology here is not entirely clear, apart from the difficulty of deciding which Artaxerxes is meant. This verse could be taken as meaning either that Nehemiah's first period as governor ended in the king's *thirty-second year*, or that his second period began then. The first alternative is suggested by 5: 14; taken by itself, this verse would favour the second. Certainty is impossible, especially in view of the vagueness of the other chronological references at this point ('before this' in verse 4 and *All this time* here are quite generalized). *Artaxerxes king of Babylon:* the title is unexpected, though the Persian kings did include this among their titles. It is comparable with the reference to 'the king of Assyria' in Ezra 6: 22 as exemplifying a tendency to identify all foreign rulers. *I asked permission from him:* the phraseology is probably a formalized way of describing a second period as governor.

7. *the wicked thing:* the details of Eliashib's action, in verse 5 and here, scarcely seem to justify such a description. Is the root of the trouble the secularizing of what should be limited to religious use, or is it that Nehemiah senses the makings of a conspiracy against his own authority? In this second mission, his actions are presented in terms of his exercise of complete authority over both secular and religious affairs.

10. *had made off:* the English expression implies some condemnation; this is not present in the Hebrew, which simply means that they had fled from Jerusalem for want of support.

11. *Why is the house of God deserted?:* the overall picture of restoration must not be allowed to obscure the dangers that still await the community if it does not remain loyal to

its obligations. Even a restored house of God might then once again be deserted.

13. *the accountant:* the translation is a curious one, since the word so rendered is the same as that used of Ezra and translated 'scribe' (Ezra 7: 6; footnote, 'doctor of the law'). None of those mentioned here can be identified with others of the same name elsewhere.

14. Prayer of this type is a characteristic feature of this chapter (cp. verses 22, 29 and 31) as a means of rounding off a section. Here it is related to the first two episodes described, both of which have shown devotion to the house of God. ✳

SABBATH OBSERVANCE

15 In those days I saw men in Judah treading winepresses on the sabbath, collecting quantities of produce and piling it on asses – wine, grapes, figs, and every kind of load, which they brought into Jerusalem on the sabbath; and I
16 protested to them about selling food on that day. Tyrians living in Jerusalem also brought in fish and all kinds of merchandise and sold them on the sabbath to the people
17 of Judah, even in Jerusalem. Then I complained to the nobles of Judah and said to them, 'How dare you profane
18 the sabbath in this wicked way? Is not this just what your fathers did, so that our God has brought all this evil on us and on this city? Now you are bringing more wrath upon
19 Israel by profaning the sabbath.' When the entrances to Jerusalem had been cleared in preparation for the sabbath, I gave orders that the gates should be shut and not opened until after the sabbath. And I appointed some of the men under me to have charge of the gates so that no load
20 might enter on the sabbath. Then on one or two occasions

the merchants and all kinds of traders camped just outside
Jerusalem, but I cautioned them. 'Why are you camping 21
in front of the city wall?' I asked. 'If you do it again, I
will take action against you.' After that they did not come
on the sabbath again. And I commanded the Levites who 22
were to purify themselves and take up duty as guards at
the gates, to ensure that the sabbath was kept holy.
Remember this also to my credit, O God, and spare me
in thy great love.

✻ Sabbath observance, though ancient, was distinctively
one of the marks of the Judaism of the later Old Testament
period. No specific law from the Pentateuch can be quoted as
dealing with the matters which led to this controversy;
rather we should see here an early stage in the process of
working out the detailed implications of the Sabbath commandment (Exod. 20: 8–11). Too great an elaboration of
such detail was an important cause of Jesus' condemnation of
the Pharisees in the gospels.

15. *In those days:* the expression is very general, here and in
verse 23; it is comparable to the 'On that day' of 12: 44 and
13: 1.

16. *Tyrians living in Jerusalem:* this provides a specific
example of the kind of danger to which the community was
exposed by contact with other races. Were the Tyrians also
to be bound by the Sabbath-commandment? Nehemiah
makes it clear by his words and subsequent action that if
they were to do business with the Jews, they must be bound
by the same laws. There may be some connection with the
requirements in 7: 3, though – as the note there has indicated
– the exact force of that passage is uncertain. ✻

FOREIGN MARRIAGES

23 In those days also I saw that some Jews had married
24 women from Ashdod, Ammon, and Moab. Half their
children spoke the language of Ashdod or of the other
25 peoples and could not speak the language of the Jews. I
argued with them and reviled them, I beat them and tore
out their hair; and I made them swear in the name of God:
'We will not marry our daughters to their sons, or take
any of their daughters in marriage for our sons or for
26 ourselves.' 'Was it not for such women', I said, 'that
King Solomon of Israel sinned? Among all the nations
there was no king like him; he was loved by his God, and
God made him king over all Israel; nevertheless even he
27 was led by foreign women into sin. Are we then to follow
your example and commit this grave offence, breaking
faith with our God by marrying foreign women?'

28   Now one of the sons of Joiada son of Eliashib the high
priest had married a daughter of Sanballat the Horonite;
29 therefore I drove him out of my presence. Remember, O
God, to their shame that they have defiled the priesthood
and the covenant of the priests[a] and the Levites.

30   Thus I purified them from everything foreign, and I
made the Levites and the priests resume the duties of their
31 office; I also made provision for the wood-offering, at
appointed times, and for the firstfruits. Remember me for
my good, O God.

☆ These verses raise again the question of foreign marriages –
the third time in these books that this point has come under

[a] *Or* priesthood.

consideration (cp. Ezra 9–10; Neh. 13: 1–3). Commentators have usually taken these as accounts of separate historical occasions and have concentrated their attention on devising theories as to why such an abuse should have arisen so frequently. But we have already observed a tendency to treat the Ezra and Nehemiah material as parallel, so that the same traditions came to relate to each of them, and it seems more likely that one tradition concerning the putting-away of foreign women has been told in varying forms. For this reason it is idle to speculate on the success of the undertaking, or to stress the difference between mere warnings given by Nehemiah in this section and apparently more drastic action taken by Ezra in Ezra 10.

23. *women from Ashdod, Ammon, and Moab:* Ammon and Moab provide a link back to the summary account in 13: 1–3; here the main concern is with Ashdod, one of the old Philistine cities south-west of Jerusalem.

24. A different aspect of the problem is here raised: the importance of a language as an indication of the survival of the distinctive identity of a people. Wales is not the only country in the modern world whose defenders have felt it imperative to insist on the preservation of the language as a means of national self-identity. What *the language of Ashdod* was is not known; it may have been a Philistine survival, or perhaps only a dialectal form of Aramaic. The phrase translated in N.E.B. *or of the other peoples* is obscure in Hebrew, and this is at best a guess; it is surprising that there is no footnote.

25. The apparently violent behaviour recorded here should be regarded as largely ritual gestures of revulsion rather than an outbreak of emotion.

26. The example of Solomon is an allusion to 1 Kings 11, where his shortcomings are set out as a preliminary to an account of the division of the kingdoms of Israel and Judah; this section has no parallel in 2 Chronicles.

28. The tension between Nehemiah and Eliashib is further

illustrated. He had been shown in verses 4–9 to be in league with one of Nehemiah's enemies, Tobiah; now he is shown to be related by marriage to the other, Sanballat. The point illustrates the double problem faced by Nehemiah (and therefore, as the Chronicler understood the situation, by all loyal Jews) – the urgency of maintaining purity and the need for watchfulness against human enemies, who might find allies even in the holy community itself. The books of Daniel and 1 Maccabees afford evidence of how acute this latter problem had become by the early second century B.C. (cp. Dan. 12; 1 Macc. 1–2). *I drove him out:* the Jewish historian Josephus, in the first century A.D., preserves what seems to be a garbled version of this story (*Antiquities* XI, 297–347), placing it in the time of Alexander the Great and linking it with the building of a rival temple by the Samaritan community on Mount Gerizim.

29. The form of the prayer here, as in 6: 14, is negative; God's remembrance must take into account unworthy as well as praiseworthy deeds.

30–1. The ending is abrupt, in the manner of many Old Testament books, but nevertheless positive, in the sense that the claim is made that, despite all the obstacles put in the way, the work of restoration had been completed and its essentials maintained against all opposition. It is for this that the plea can finally be advanced on Nehemiah's behalf: *Remember me for my good, O God.* ✲

WHY SHOULD WE READ THESE BOOKS TODAY?

There are likely to be two reasons for people wishing to read these books today. First, for students of the bible at all academic levels, they tell us something of a period about which we should otherwise know little, of a time when the fortunes of the people of God seemed to be at a low ebb, but which was nevertheless far from hopeless; and the Chronicler, though often critical of the people, is never without hope and never allows them to forget the destiny to which they were called. The commentary has tried to show that detailed historical reconstruction is often more difficult than might at first sight appear, but despite this we still get a vivid picture of the state of affairs in Judah between the sixth and the fourth centuries B.C.

The second reason will be of concern especially to those who are themselves practising Jews or Christians. Each makes the claim to be in some sense the people of God. What does such a claim mean in terms both of identity with, and of separation from, the surrounding world? It is a question to which there is no easy answer, and it would be foolish to claim that these books provide an answer that we should wish to follow, for example in respect of mixed marriages. Nevertheless they force our attention to the question: what does the claim to be the people of God mean, and how is such a people to be differentiated from those, sometimes sympathetic, sometimes hostile, among whom they live?

A NOTE ON FURTHER READING

The historical background of the period dealt with in these books will be found set out in M. Noth, *The History of Israel*, 2nd ed. (A. & C. Black, 1960), J. Bright, *A History of Israel*, 2nd ed. (S.C.M. Press, 1972) and S. Herrmann, *A History of Israel in Old Testament Times* (S.C.M. Press, 1975).

Other commentaries which may be consulted include those by P. R. Ackroyd, *I and II Chronicles, Ezra and Nehemiah*, Torch Commentary (S.C.M. Press, 1973), which has the advantage of looking at the whole of the Chronicler's work; J. M. Myers, *Ezra and Nehemiah*, Anchor Bible (Doubleday, New York, 1965), with a very full introduction and several statistical appendices; and L. H. Brockington, *Ezra, Nehemiah and Esther*, New Century Bible (Nelson (now Oliphant), 1969), with much detailed information about personal names.

APPENDIX

WEIGHTS AND COINS

| | heavy (Phoenician) standard | | | light (Babylonian) standard | | |
	shekel	mina	talent	shekel	mina	talent
shekel	1	...	...	1	...	...
mina	50	1	...	60	1	...
talent	3,000	60	1	3,600	60	1

The 'gerah' was $\frac{1}{20}$ of the sacred or heavy shekel and probably $\frac{1}{24}$ of the light shekel.

The 'sacred shekel' according to tradition was identical with the heavy shekel; while the 'shekel of the standard recognized by merchants' (Gen. 23: 16) was perhaps a weight stamped with its value as distinct from one not so stamped and requiring to be weighed on the spot.

Recent discoveries of hoards of objects stamped with their weights suggest that the shekel may have weighed approximately 11·5 grammes towards the end of the Hebrew monarchy, but nothing shows whether this is the light or the heavy shekel; and much variety, due partly to the worn or damaged state of the objects and partly to variations in local standards, increases the difficulty of giving a definite figure.

Coins are not mentioned before the exile. Only the 'daric' (1 Chron. 29: 7) and the 'drachma' (Ezra 2: 69; Neh. 7: 70–2), if this is a distinct coin, are found in the Old Testament; the former is said to have been a month's pay for a soldier in the Persian army, while the latter will have been the Greek silver drachma, estimated at approximately 4·4 grammes. The 'shekel' of this period (Neh. 5: 15) as a coin was probably the Graeco-Persian *siglos* weighing 5·6 grammes.

MEASURES OF CAPACITY

liquid measures	equivalences	dry measures
'log'	1 'log'	...
...	4 'log'	'kab'
...	7½ 'log'	'omer'
'hin'	12 'log'	...
...	24 'log'	'seah'
'bath'	72 'log'	'ephah'
'kor'	720 'log'	'homer' or 'kor'

According to ancient authorities the Aebrew 'log' was of the same capacity as the Roman *sextarius*; this according to the best available evidence was equivalent to 0·99 pint of the English standard.

INDEX

INDEX